Anson Randolph

The chamber of peace and other religious poems

Anson Randolph

The chamber of peace and other religious poems

ISBN/EAN: 9783337119041

Printed in Europe, USA, Canada, Australia, Japan

Cover: Foto ©Lupo / pixelio.de

More available books at **www.hansebooks.com**

The Chamber of Peace

AND

OTHER RELIGIOUS POEMS.

Selected and Edited

By the Compiler of "THE CHANGED CROSS," "THE SHADOW OF THE ROCK," etc.

"The Pilgrim they ...
the sunrising.
"The name of the c...

NE...
ANSON D. ...
770 BROAD...

COPYRIGHT, 1874, BY
ANSON D. F. RANDOLPH & COMPANY.

ROBERT RUTTER,
BINDER,
84 BEEKMAN STREET, N. Y.

EDWARD O. JENKINS,
PRINTER AND STEREOTYPER,
20 NORTH WILLIAM ST., N. Y.

PUBLISHER'S NOTE.

This collection of Poems, selected and arranged by the compiler of "THE CHANGED CROSS" and "THE SHADOW OF THE ROCK," it is hoped will prove acceptable to those with whom the other volumes have so long been favorites.

The Poems have been gathered from many sources; largely from the newspaper and magazine; and the names of the authors, so far as they could be ascertained, will be found in the Index.

NOVEMBER, 1874.

CARRARA.

A SHIP unlading, busy sea-brown hands
    Are lifting blocks of marble, one by one;
Quarried where fair Carrara's golden sands
    And purple hills lie sleeping in the sun.

The workman earned his share of daily bread;
    The merchant counted up his gains in gold;
" What unwrought statues there," the artist said,
    " What lines of beauty, rare and manifold!

" What grace and glory from these blocks shall spring!
    What light shall clothe them in a little while!
This shapeless block, in beauty blossoming,
    Shall breathe high thoughts or wear an angel's smile."

O Lives that in a martyr-army stand,
    May God's sweet message come to you and me.
We are the marble, His the Sculptor-Hand
    That fashions us for all eternity.

We only feel the pain His chastenings give;
    The sharp incisions only can we see.
And He alone, by whom we move and live,
    He sees the hidden glory that shall be.

He sees the glory without spot or stain,
    The spiritual beauty all unpriced;
And in His love, He sends each stroke of pain
    To make us like our dear Lord Jesus Christ.

O God of Love, give us calm pitying eyes
    And sweetest patience. Let us also see
The glory and the grace that underlies
    Each shapeless mass that waits a touch from Thee.

THE CHAMBER OF PEACE

AND OTHER

RELIGIOUS POEMS.

THE CHAMBER OF PEACE.

"The Pilgrim they laid in a large upper chamber, facing the sun-rising. The name of the chamber was Peace."—
BUNYAN'S PILGRIM'S PROGRESS.

AFTER the burden and heat of the day,
   The starry calm of night;
After the rough and toilsome way,
   A sleep in the robe of white.

O blessèd Pilgrim! we see thy face
   As an angel's face might seem,
For, lying pale in that shadowy place,
   Thou dreamest a golden dream.

The stars are watching the sleeping saint,
   And lighting the sleeping brow;
But the light of the stars is cold and faint
   To the glory he dreameth now:

For the things that are hid from waking eyes
   Shine clear to the veilèd sight ;
From the chamber dim where the Pilgrim lies
   We can watch the fountains of light.

The journey is over, the fight is fought,
   He hath seen the Home of his love ;
And the smile on the dreamer's face is caught
   From the land of smiles above.

We also have sometimes lain asleep
   In the blessèd Chamber of Peace ;
Too weary to wrestle, or watch, or weep,
   For a while the struggle must cease—

We give thanks for the weakness that makes us lie
   So helpless and calm for a while ;
The roar of the battle goes hoarsely by,
   And we hear it, in dreams, with a smile.

Oh, sweet is the slumber wherewith the King
   Hath caused the weary to rest !
For, sleeping, we hear the angels sing,
   We lean on the Master's breast.

Thou hast another Chamber, dear Lord—
   The secret place of peace,
Where Thy precious ones are safely stored,
   When their weary wanderings cease :

THE CHAMBER OF PEACE.

After the burden and heat of the day,
   The starry calm of night;
After the rough and toilsome way,
   A sleep in the robe of white.

The sacred Chamber is still and wide,
   You listen in vain for a breath;
And pale lie the sleepers, side by side,
   In the cold moonlight of death.

No sighs are heard in the shadowy place,
   No voices of them that weep;
They have fought the fight, and finished the
      race—
   God giveth them rest in sleep.

Are they dreaming, the sleepers pale and still?
   For their faces are rapt and calm,
As though they were treading the Holy Hill,
   And hearkening the angels' psalm:

The things that were hid from waking eyes
   Shine clear to the veiled sight;
In the last deep sleep the Pilgrims rise,
   To walk on the shores of Light.

Oh, sweet is the slumber wherewith the King
   Hath caused the weary to rest!
For, sleeping, they hear the angels sing,
   They lean on the Master's breast.

And sweet is the Chamber, silent and wide,
   Where lingers the holy smile
Of a wayfaring Man, who turned aside
   To rest, long ago, for a while:

He had suffered a sorrow which none may tell,
   He had purchased a Gift unpriced;
When his work was over the moonlight fell
   On the sleeping face of Christ:

The face of a Victor, dead and crowned,
   With a smile divinely fair:
The saints and martyrs sleeping around
   Were stirred as He entered there:*

His very Name is as ointment poured
   On the moonlight pale to-night;
And the Chamber is sweet to Thy servants, Lord,
   For the scent of Thy raiment white.

The silent Chamber faceth the east,
   Faceth the dawn of the day,
And the shining feet of our great High Priest
   Shall break through the shadows gray.

---

   * "And the graves were opened, and many bodies of the saints which slept arose."—MATT. xxvii. 52.

The golden dawn of the Day of God
   Shall smite on the sealèd eyes;
The trumpet's sound shall thunder around,
   The dreamers shall wake and rise.

The night is over, the sleep is slept,
   They are called from the shadowy place;
The Pilgrims stand in the glorious land,
   And gaze on the Master's face.

TIRED.

"Does the road wind uphill all the way?
      Yes, to the very end."
So tired!—I fain would rest.
But, Lord, thou knowest best,
      I wait on Thee.
I will toil on from day to day,
Bearing my cross, and only pray
      To follow Thee.

So tired: my friends are gone
And I am left alone,
      And days are sad.
Lord Jesus, *Thou* wilt bear my load
Along this steep and weary road,
      And make me glad.

So tired: my heart is low,
Shadows of coming woe
      Around me fall.
And memories of sins long wept
And hopes denied that long have slept,
      Arise and call.

So tired: yet I would work
For Thee!—Lord, hast Thou work
      Even for me?
Small things—which others, hurrying on
In Thy blest service, swift and strong,
      Might never see?

So tired: yet I might reach
A flower to cheer and teach
      Some sadder heart;
Or for parched lips perhaps might bring
One cup of water from the spring,
      Ere I depart.

So tired: yet it were sweet
Some faltering tender feet
      To help and guide,
Thy little ones whose steps are slow,
I should not weary them, I know,
      Nor roughly chide.

So tired! Lord, Thou wilt come
To take me to my home,
      So long desired:

Only Thy grace and mercy send,
That I may serve Thee to the end,
   Though I am tired.

IN THE EVENING.

All day the wind had howled along the leas,
   All day the wind had swept across the plain,
All day on rustling grass and waving trees
   Had fallen "the useful trouble of the rain."
All day beneath the low-hung dreary sky
The dripping earth had cowered sullenly.

At last the wind had sobbed itself to rest,
   At last to weary calmness sank the storm,
A crimson line gleamed sudden in the west,
   Where golden flecks rose wavering into form.
A hushed revival heralded the night,
And with the evening time awoke the light.

The rosy color flushed the long gray waves;
   The rosy color tinged the mountains' brown;
And where the old church watched the village graves,
   Wooed to a passing blush the yew-trees' frown.
Bird, beast, and flower, relenting nature knew,
And one pale star rose shimmering in the blue.

So, to a life long crushed in heavy grief,
  So, to a path long darkened by despair,
The slow sad hours bring touches of relief,
  Whispers of hope, and strength of trustful
      prayer.
"Tarry his leisure," God of love and might,
And with the evening time there will be light!

SORROW.

UPON my lips she laid her touch divine,
    And merry speech and careless laughter
      died;
She fixed her melancholy eyes on mine,
    And would not be denied.

I saw the west wind loose his cloudlets white,
  In flocks careering through the April sky;
I could not sing, though joy was at its height,
    For she stood silent by.

I watched the lovely evening fade away—
  A mist was lightly drawn across the stars;
She broke my quiet dream—I heard her say,
    "Behold your prison bars.

"Earth's gladness shall not satisfy your soul,
  This beauty of the world in which you live;

The crowning grace that sanctifies the whole,
    That I alone can give."

I heard, and shrunk away from her afraid,
    But still she held me, and would still abide,
Youth's bounding pulses slackened and obeyed
    With slowly-ebbing tide.

"Look thou beyond the evening sky," she said,
    "Beyond the changing splendors of the day.
Accept the pain, the weariness, the dread,
    Accept, and bid me stay."

I turned, and clasped her close, with sudden strength,
    And slowly, sweetly, I became aware
Within my arms God's angels stood at length,
    White-robed, and calm, and fair.

And now I look beyond the evening star,
    Beyond the changing splendors of the day,
Knowing the pain He sends more precious far,
    More beautiful than they.

NIGHT AND DAY.

THE day is Thine—
    The long, bright summer day,
From the first dawning light till evening closes,
And all its merry birds and blooming roses,
    And all its golden beauty bid us say,
        The day, O Lord, is Thine.

    And life's brief day
  Is also Thine, when we
Must work, while light doth last, for our dear
        Master.
O that our sluggish feet could travel faster,
    And we with readier service give to Thee
        Our life's fast-fleeting day!

        The night is Thine—
  The long, dark winter's night,
Hushing our birds to sleep, our flowers concealing;
But, by its hosts of glowing stars, revealing,
    Through the deep sky, Thy glory and Thy
        might.
        The night, O Lord, is Thine!

        That darker night
    Is also Thine, O Lord,
When Thou sweet sleep to Thy beloved givest;

For while they needs must sleep, Thou ever
livest,
  And o'er Thy dear ones keepest watch and
ward,
    Till darkness ends in light.

"DYING, YET BEHOLD WE LIVE."

A SHIP, full laden, left her native port,
  To plough the waves, and seek another
clime;
Her sails were set, and gallant ranks of men,
  If the wind failed, would with their oars keep
time.

Her port she left, but on a troubled main,
  Her every sinew, every nerve, she strained;
Yet wooed the breezes, spread her sails in vain—
  She sped not on her way, nor land she gained.

Then rose the pilot: "Heed my words," he
cried;
  "Too many a weighty gift this ship ye gave;
Cast this and that away, and she shall ride
  Lightly, and unencumbered, o'er the wave."

With niggard hand, reluctantly they drew
  Some trifles from her breast, and in the sea
They one by one these secret treasures threw,
  And saw them sink in its immensity.

Yet still, as if held back by leaden hands,
   The ship no progress made, and so once more,
The pilot, working her from off the sands,
   Made the same plaint his voice had made before.

Then one by one her treasures left her deck,
   To be by yawning, briny jaws consumed,
And 'mid fierce winds and storms, an empty wreck,
   Went staggering into port, condemned and doomed.

And yet the pilot from the master won
   Plaudits and welcomes that his zeal repaid,
For on his ear there fell the glad well-done,
   Who, faithful to his trust, no trust betrayed.

Thus, O my soul, thy Pilot made thy way
   Straight to the haven where thou fain wouldst be;
Nor feared to rob thee, cut thy spars away,
   Knowing the Master only cared for thee.

For thee, dismantled, empty, good for naught,
   For thee, who unto him no treasure bore;
Then ride at anchor, tempest-tossed, distraught,
   For thou hast touched at an eternal shore!

MATER DOLOROSA.

BECAUSE of little low-laid heads all cov-
  ered
    With golden hair,
Forevermore all fair young brows to me
    A halo wear:
I kiss them reverently,—alas! I know
    The stains I bear.

Because of dear but close-shut holy eyes
    Of heaven's own blue,
All little eyes do fill my own with tears,
    Whate'er their hue;
And motherly I gaze their innocent
    Clear depths into.

Because of little pallid lips which once
    My name did call,
No childish voice, in vain appeal, upon
    My ear doth fall.
I count it all my joy their joys to share
    And sorrows small.

Because of little dimpled, cherished hands
    Which folded lie,
All little hands henceforth to me do have
    A pleading cry;
I clasp them as they were small wandering birds
    Lured home to fly.

Because of little death-cold feet, for earth's
        Rough roads unmeet,
I'd journey leagues to save from sin or harm
        Such little feet;
And count the lowliest service done for them
        So sacred—sweet!

BEYOND.

BEYOND life's toils and cares,
    Its hopes and joys, its weariness and
        sorrow,
Its sleepless nights, its days of smiles and tears,
Will be a long sweet life, unmarked by years,
        One bright, unending morrow!

        Beyond Time's troubled stream,
Beyond the chilling waves of death's dark river,
Beyond life's lowering clouds and fitful gleams,
Its dark realities and brighter dreams,—
        A beautiful forever.

        No aching hearts are there,
No tear-dimmed eye, no form by sickness
        wasted,
No cheek grown pale through penury or care,
No spirits crushed beneath the woes they bear,
        No sighs for bliss untasted.

BEYOND.

No sad farewell is heard,
No lonely wail for loving ones departed,
No dark remorse is there o'er memories stirred,
No smile of scorn, no harsh or cruel word
    To grieve the broken-hearted.

No long dark night is there,
No light from sun or silvery moon is given;
But Christ, the Lamb of God, all bright and fair,
Illumes the city with effulgence rare,
    The glorious light of heaven!

No mortal eye hath seen
The glories of that land beyond that river,
Its crystal lakes, its fields of living green,
Its fadeless flowers, and the unchanging sheen
    Around the throne forever.

Ear hath not heard the song
Of rapturous praise within that shining portal;
No heart of man hath dreamed what joys belong
To that redeemed and happy blood-washed
    throng,
    All glorious and immortal.

A LITTLE WAY.

A LITTLE way—I know it is not far
To that dear home where my belovèd are;
And yet my faith grows weaker as I stand
A poor, lone pilgrim in a dreary land,
Where present pain the future bliss obscures.
And still my heart sits, like a bird, upon
The empty nest, and mourns its treasures gone;
      Plumed for their flight,
      And vanished quite.
Ah, me! where is the comfort?—though I say
They have but journeyed on a little way!

A little way—at times they seem so near,
Their voices ever murmur at my ear;
To all my duties loving presence lend,
And with sweet ministry my steps attend,
And bring my soul the luxury of tears.
'Twas here we met and parted company;
Why should their gain be such a grief to me?
      This sense of loss!
      This heavy cross!
Dear Saviour, take the burden off, I pray,
And show me heaven is but—a little way.

These sombre robes, these saddened faces, all
The bitterness, the pain of death, recall;

Ah! let me turn my face where'er I may,
I see the traces of a sure decay;
And parting takes the marrow out of life.
Secure in bliss, we hold the golden chain
Which death, with scarce a warning, snaps in
        twain ;
      And nevermore
      Shall time restore
The broken links; 'twas only yesterday
They vanished from our sight—a little way.

A little way!—this sentence I repeat,
Hoping and longing to extract some sweet
To mingle with the bitter ; from Thy hand
I take the cup I cannot understand,
And in my weakness give myself to Thee!
Although it seems so very, very far
To that dear home where my belovèd are,
      I know, I know
      It is not so;
Oh, give me faith to feel it when I say
That they are gone—gone but a little way!

THE LAND BEYOND THE SEA.

THE land beyond the sea!
    When will life's task be o'er?
When shall we reach that soft blue shore

O'er the dark strait, whose billows foam and
    roar?
    When shall we come to thee,
    Calm land beyond the sea?

    The land beyond the sea!
How close it often seems,
When flushed with evening's peaceful gleams;
And the wistful heart looks o'er the strait and
    dreams!
    It longs to fly to thee,
    Calm land beyond the sea!

    The land beyond the sea!
Sometimes distinct and near,
It grows upon the eye and ear,
And the gulf narrows to a thread-like mere;
    We seem half way to thee,
    Calm land beyond the sea!

    The land beyond the sea!
Sometimes across the strait,
Like a draw-bridge to a castle gate,
The slanting sunbeams lie, and seem to wait
    For us to pass to thee,
    Calm land beyond the sea!

    The land beyond the sea!
Oh, how the lapsing years,

'Mid our not unsubmissive tears,
Have borne, now singly, now in fleets, the biers
    Of those we love, to thee,
    Calm land beyond the sea!

    The land beyond the sea!
How dark our present home!
By the dull beach and sullen foam
How wearily, how drearily we roam,
    With arms outstretched to thee,
    Calm land beyond the sea!

    The land beyond the sea!
When will our toil be done?
Slow-footed years! more swiftly run
Into the gold of that unsetting sun!
    Home-sick we are for thee,
    Calm land beyond the sea!

    The land beyond the sea!
Why fadest thou in light?
Why art thou better seen towards night?
Dear land! look always plain, look always
    bright,
    That we may gaze on thee,
    Calm land beyond the sea!

    The land beyond the sea!
Sweet is thine endless rest,

But sweeter far that Father's breast
Upon thy shores eternally possessed
    For Jesus reigns o'er thee,
    Calm land beyond the sea!

THE SECRET.

THE winds are raging o'er the upper ocean,
    And billows wild contend with angry roar.
'Tis said, far down beneath the wild commotion,
    That peaceful stillness reigneth evermore.

Far, far beneath, the noise of tempest dieth,
    And silver waves chime ever peacefully,
And no rude storm, how fierce soe'er he flieth,
    Disturbs the Sabbath of that deeper sea.

So to the soul that knows Thy love, O Purest,
    There is a temple peaceful evermore;
And all the bubble of life's angry voices
    Die in hushed stillness at its sacred door.

Far, far away the noise of passion dieth,
    And loving thoughts rise ever peacefully,
And no rude storm, how fierce soe'er he flieth,
    Disturbs that deeper rest, O Lord, in Thee.

O rest of rests! O peace serene, eternal!
    Thou ever livest, and thou changest never!
And in the secret of Thy presence dwelleth
    Fullness of joy, forever and forever.

"SO HE BRINGETH THEM UNTO THEIR DESIRED HAVEN."

Psalm cvii. 30.

"SO!"—through storms and darkness,
  Through great waters deep,
Through the cloud whose black embraces
  Hidden sunbeams keep:
 So, He brings His chosen there
 To the Haven safe and fair!

"*So!*"—through fierce winds blowing,
  Through rough desert ways,
Through long nights whose dreary darkness
  Reaches o'er the days:
 So, He brings them Home at last,
 Safe from every stormy blast!

"*So!*"—through cares and trials;
  Through temptations strong,
Through dead hopes, whose joyous blossoms
  Have been waited long:
 So, He brings His chosen Home,
 Nevermore to sadly roam!

"*So!*"—by tears and longings,
  By the spirit's strife,
By the hands outreaching vainly
  Toward this empty life:

So, He brings them Home to share
In His perfect " fullness " there !

" *So !* "—by small, slow footsteps,
    By the daily cross,
By the heart's unspoken yearning,
    By its grief and loss :
So, He brings them Home to rest
With the victors, crowned and blest !

" *So !* "—by scattered ruins,
    By sweet links unbound,
By fair blossoms all unheeded,
    Trampled on the ground :
So, He brings them Home to Him,
Where no cloud their joy can dim !

" *So !* "—oh, weary pilgrim,
    'Tis the Master's way,
And it leadeth surely, surely,
    Unto endless day !
Doubt not, fear not—gladly go ;
He will bring thee heavenward *so !*

TRUST.

I KNOW not if the dark or bright
    Shall be my lot ;
If that wherein my hope delight
    Be best or not.

TRUST.

It may be mine to drag for years
      Toil's heavy chain ;
Or day and night my meat be tears
      On bed of pain.

Dear faces may surround my hearth
      With smiles and glee ;
Or I may dwell alone, and mirth
      Be strange to me.

My bark is wafted to the strand
      By breath divine,
And on the helm there rests a hand
      Other than mine.

One who has known in storms to sail,
      I have on board ;
Above the raging of the gale
      I hear my Lord

He holds me with the billow's might—
      I shall not fall ;
If sharp, 'tis short ; if long, 'tis light ;
      He tempers all.

Safe to the land—safe to the land,
      The end is this ;
And then with Him go hand in hand
      Far into bliss.

THE WILL OF GOD.

ALL goeth but God's will!
    The fairest garden flower
    Fades after its brief hour
Of brightness. . Still,
This is but God's good-will.

    All goeth but God's will!
The brightest, dearest day,
Doth swiftest pass away,
    And darkest night
    Succeeds the vision bright.

    But still strong-hearted be,
Yea, though the night be drear—
How sad and long soe'er
    Its gloom may be,
    This darkness, too, shall flee.

    Weep not yon grave beside!
Dear friends, he is not gone;
God's angels soon this stone
    Shall roll aside,
    Yea, Death shall not abide!

    Earth's anguish, too, shall go.
O then, be strong, my soul.!
When sorrows o'er thee roll,

Be still, and know
'Tis God's will worketh so.

Dear Lord and God, incline
Thine ear unto my call!
O grant me that in all,
  This will of mine
  May still be one with Thine!

Teach me to answer still,
Whate'er my lot may be,
To all thou sendest me,
  Of good, or ill;
  " All goeth as God will."

'TIS ALL THE SAME TO ME.

'TIS all the same to me—
  Sorrow, and strife, and pining want, and pain!
Whate'er it is, it cometh all from Thee,
  And 'tis not mine to doubt Thee or complain.

Thou knowest what is best;
  And who but Thee, O God, hath power to know?
In Thy great will my trusting heart shall rest
  Beneath that will my humble head shall bow.

Then what Thou pleasest send;
  To order all my destiny is Thine.
With Thee, in all Thy purposes, to blend
  In unity of heart, let that be mine.

No questions will I ask,
  Do what Thou wilt, my Father and my God;
Obedience is my consecrated task,
  Though Thou should'st lead me where Thy martyrs trod.

Alike, all pleases well,
  Since living faith hath made it understood—
Within the shadowy folds of sorrow dwell
The seeds of life and everlasting good.

THE TWO CITIES.

ON the dusky shores of evening, stretched in shining peace it lies,
City built of clouds and sunshine—wonder of the Western skies.

While I watch and long for pinions, thitherward to take my flight,
Slow the ærial city fadeth, and vanisheth from sight.

Ruby dome and silver temple, circling wall of amethyst,
Fall in silence, leaving only purple ruin hung with mist.

Darkness gathers, Eastward, Westward; stronger waxeth my desire,
Reaching through celestial spaces, glittering as with rain of fire,

To the city set with jasper, having twelve foundations fair,
Flashing from their jeweled splendor every color soft and rare.

Twelve in number are its gateways—numbered by the seer of old—
Every gate a pearl most lustrous—and its streets are paved with gold.

In the midst, in dazzling whiteness, lightens the eternal throne;
From it flows the living water—round it gleams an emerald zone.

Luscious fruits and balmy odors, healing leaves and cooling shade,
Either side the life-tree sheddeth, by sweet storms of music swayed.

O thou grand, untempled city, seen by John in
    vision bright,
Glory-flooded, needing neither sun by day nor
    moon by night.

Filled forever and forever by the shining light
    of Him
Who redeemed the world, and sitteth throned
    between the seraphim!

Through thy lovely gates the nations of the
    saved in triumph stream,
Chanting praise above all praises—love of love
    their holy theme!

They no more shall thirst or hunger—they no
    more with heat shall faint;
Christ for tears will give them gladness—bliss-
    ful rest for sore complaint.

"Blessed they who do His bidding!" cries the
    angel, day and night;
They shall find abundant entrance—they shall
    walk with Him in white!

HE KNOWETH ALL.

"He knoweth the way that I take."—JOB xxiii. 10.

THE twilight falls, the night is near,
   I fold my work away,
And kneel to One who bends to hear
   The story of the day.

The old, old story, yet I kneel
   To tell it at Thy call;
And cares grow lighter as I feel
   That Jesus knows them all.

Yes, all! The morning and the night,
   The joy, the grief, the loss,
The roughened path, the sunbeam bright,
   The hourly thorn and cross.

Thou knowest all—I lean my head;
   My weary eyelids close;
Content and glad awhile to tread
   This path, since Jesus knows!

And He has loved me! All my heart
   With answering love is stirred,
And every anguished pain and smart
   Finds healing in the Word.

So here I lay me down to rest,
  As nightly shadows fall,
And lean confiding on His breast
  Who knows and pities all!

WHAT THEN?

WHAT then? Why then another pilgrim song,
  And then a hush of rest, divinely granted;
And then a thirsty stage, (Ah, me, so long!)
  And then a brook, just where it most is wanted.

What then? The pitching of the evening tent;
  And then, perchance, a pillow rough and thorny;
And then some sweet and tender message, sent
  To cheer the faint one for to-morrow's journey.

What then? The wailing of the midnight wind;
  A feverish sleep, a heart oppressed and aching;
And then a little water-cruse to find
  Close by my pillow, ready for my waking.

What then? I am not careful to inquire:
  I know there will be tears, and fears, and sorrow;
But then a loving Saviour drawing nigher,
  And saying,—I will answer for the morrow.

What then? For all my sins, His pardoning grace;
  For all my wants and woes, His loving-kindness;
For darkest shades, the shining of God's face,
  And Christ's own hand to lead me in my blindness.

What then? A shadowy valley, lone and dim,
  And then a deep and darkly rolling river;
And then a flood of light, a seraph hymn,
  And God's own smile forever and forever!

THE LOVED AND LOST.

"THE loved and lost!" why do we call them lost,
  Because we miss them from our onward road?
God's unseen angel o'er our pathway crossed,
Looked on us all, and loving them the most,
  Straightway relieved them from life's weary load.

THE LOVED AND LOST.

They are not lost; they are within the door
   That shuts out loss, and every hurtful thing—
With angels bright, and loved ones gone before,
In their Redeemer's presence evermore,
   And God Himself their Lord, and Judge, and
      King.

And this we call a loss; O selfish sorrow
   Of selfish hearts! O we of little faith!
Let us look round, some argument to borrow
Why we in patience should await the morrow
   That surely must succeed this night of death.

Ay, look upon this dreary desert path,
   The thorns and thistles whereso'er we turn;
What trials and what tears, what wrongs and
      wrath,
What struggles and what strife the journey
      hath!
   They have escaped from these; and lo! we
      mourn.

Ask the poor sailor, when the wreck is done,
   Who with his treasure strove the shore to
      reach,
While with the raging waves he battled on—
Was it not joy, where every joy seemed gone,
   To see his loved ones landed on the beach?

A poor wayfarer, leading by the hand
   A little child, had halted by the well
To wash from off her feet the clinging sand,
And tell the tired boy of that bright land
   Where, this long journey past, they longed
     to dwell.

When lo! the Lord, who many mansions had,
   Drew near, and looked upon the suffering
     twain,
Then pitying spake, "Give me the little lad:
In strength renewed, and glorious beauty clad,
   I'll bring him with me, when I come again."

Did she make answer selfishly and wrong—
   "Nay, but the woes I feel, he too must
     share!"
Or rather, bursting into grateful song,
She went her way rejoicing, and made strong
   To struggle on, since he was freed from care.

We will do likewise; death hath made no
     breach
   In love and sympathy, in hope and trust;
No outward sign or sound our ears can reach;
But there's an inward, spiritual speech
   That greets us still, though mortal tongues
     be dust.

It bids us do the work that they laid down—
   Take up the song where they broke off the
      strain;
So journeying till we reach the heavenly town,
Where are laid up our treasures and our crown,
   And our lost loved ones will be found again.

HEAVIER THE CROSS.

[From the German.]

HEAVIER the cross, the nearer Heaven;
   No cross without, no God within—
Death, judgment from the heart are driven
   Amid the world's false glare and din.
     Oh! happy he with all his loss,
      Whom God hath set beneath the cross.

Heavier the cross, the better Christian;
   This is the touch-stone God applies.
How many a garden would be wasting,
   Unwet by showers from weeping eyes!
     The gold by fire is purified;
     The Christian is by trouble tried.

Heavier the cross, the stronger faith;
   The loaded palm strikes deeper root;
The vine-juice sweetly issueth
   When men have pressed the clustered fruit;

And courage grows where dangers come,
  Like pearls beneath the salt sea foam.

Heavier the cross, the heartier prayer;
  The bruisèd reeds most fragrant are;
If sky and wind were always fair,
  The sailor would not watch the star;
    And David's psalms had ne'er been sung,
    If grief his heart had never wrung.

Heavier the cross, the more aspiring;
  From vales we climb to mountain crest;
The pilgrim of the desert tiring,
  Longs for the Canaan of his rest.
    The dove has here no rest in sight,
    And to the ark she wings her flight.

Heavier the cross, the easier dying;
  Death is a friendlier face to see;
To life's decay one bids defying,
  From life's distress one then is free.
    The cross sublimely lifts our faith
    To Him who triumphed over death.

Thou crucified, the cross I carry,
  The longer, may it dearer be;
And lest I faint while here I tarry,
  Implant Thou such a heart in me
    That faith, hope, love, may flourish there,
    Till for the cross my crown I wear.

"ONE OF THE SWEET OLD CHAPTERS."

ONE of the sweet old chapters
   After a day like this—
The day brought tears and trouble,
   The evening brings no kiss.

No rest in the aims I long for—
   Rest, and refuge, and home;
Grieved, and lonely, and weary,
   Unto the Book I come.

One of the sweet old chapters—
   The love that blossoms through
His care of the birds and lilies,
   Out in the meadow dew.

His evening lies soft around them;
   Their faith is simply to be.
Oh, hushed by the tender lesson,
   My God, let me rest in Thee!

SLEEP.

"So He giveth His beloved sleep."—PSALM cxxvii. 2.

HE sees when their footsteps falter, when
   their hearts grow weak and faint;
He marks when their strength is failing, and
   listens to each complaint;

He bids them rest for a season, for the path-
    way has grown too steep;
And folded in fair green pastures,
       He giveth His loved ones sleep.

Like weary and worn-out children, that sigh
    for the daylight's close,
He knows that they oft are longing for home
    and its sweet repose;
So He calls them in from their labors ere the
    shadows around them creep,
And silently watching o'er them,
       He giveth His loved ones sleep.

He giveth it, oh! so gently, as a mother will
    hush to rest
The babe that she softly pillows so tenderly on
    her breast;
Forgotten are now the trials and sorrows that
    made them weep;
For with many a soothing promise
       He giveth His loved ones sleep.

He giveth it! Friends the dearest can never
    this boon bestow;
But He touches the drooping eyelids, and placid
    the features grow;

Their foes may gather about them, and storms
    may round them sweep,
But, guarding them safe from danger,
    He giveth His loved ones sleep.

All dread of the distant future, all fears that
    oppressed to-day,
Like mists, that clear in the sunlight, have
    noiselessly passed away;
Nor call, nor clamor can rouse them from
    slumbers so pure and deep,
For only His voice can reach them
    Who giveth His loved ones sleep.

Weep not that their toils are over, weep not
    that their race is run;
God grant we may rest as calmly when our
    work, like theirs, is done!
Till then we would yield with gladness our
    treasures to Him to keep,
And rejoice in the sweet assurance,
    He giveth His loved ones sleep.

THE GATHERING HOME.

THEY are gathering homeward from every
    land,
        One by one,
As their weary feet touch the shining strand,
        One by one.

Their brows are enclosed in a golden crown,
Their travel-stained garments are all laid down,
And clothed in white garments they rest on the mead,
Where the Lamb doth love His chosen to lead,
    One by one.

Before they rest they pass through the strife,
    One by one.
Through the waters of death they enter life,
    One by one.
To some are the floods of the river still,
As they ford on their way to the heavenly hill;
To others the waves run fiercely and wild,
Yet they reach the home of the undefiled,
    One by one.

We, too, shall come to the river side,
    One by one.
We are nearer its waters each eventide,
    One by one.
We can hear the noise and dash of the stream
Now, and again, through our life's deep dream;
Sometimes the floods all the banks overflow,
Sometimes in ripples and small waves go,
    One by one.

Jesus, Redeemer, we look unto Thee,
    One by one.

We lift up our voices tremblingly,
          One by one.
The waves of the river are dark and cold,
We know not the place where our feet may
    hold;
Thou who didst pass through in deep midnight,
Strengthen us, send us the staff and the light,
          One by one.

Plant Thou Thy feet beside as we tread,
          One by one.
On Thee let us lean each drooping head,
          One by one.
Let but Thy strong arm around us be twined,
We shall cast our fears and cares to the wind,
Saviour, Redeemer, with Thee full in view,
Smilingly, gladsomely, shall we pass through,
          One by one.

OVER MY DEAD.

NOW while Thy hand is on me, O my God,
    Keep common thoughts apart:
Let the full meaning of Thy heavy rod
    Sink in my inmost heart.

I will not give my eyes to dainty sight,
    Nor lips to dainty food.

Disdain, thou heaven-taught soul, these near
    delights,
        And make thy God thy good.

Into Thy secret place, O Lord, I come,
        Awe-struck, but not afraid.
My straying soul shall find herself at home
        Within that solemn shade.

Nor worldly glare nor gloom assails my eyes
        In that serene abode;
The far-off sound of worldly tumult dies;
        I hide myself in God.

O Jesus! Saviour, who from all the gloom
        Of mortal sin and strife,
Didst pierce a doorway through the rocky tomb
        Straight into endless life:

Hold Thou my hand; I tread that rugged floor
        With these weak feet of clay;
My dead I follow, as they walk before
        Into eternal day.

Set angel guards behind me; roll the stone,
        And keep my spirit in;
Till I walk forth new-made, and not alone;
        Nor lose what I have seen.

The lustre of Thy risen presence, Lord,
    Shall be my daily light :
The steadfast hope of Thy approving word
    Shall guide my steps aright.

Grant me the comforts of a soul forgiven,
    And wisdom, Lord, to see
How mortal man lives on the verge of heaven,
    By living unto Thee.

GOING TO SLEEP.

OH ! come to the bedside in silence ;
    Our mother is going to sleep !
We'll watch in the hush of the twilight,
    And praise God while we weep,
        While we weep.

Her bright hair has long since been silvered,
    Our own has grown faded and gray ;
There's no light 'neath her tremulous eyelids,
    And now she is passing away,
        Passing away.

Oh ! the life-long love of a mother,
    Is a guerdon to guard and to keep ;
And we'll cherish its memory closer,
    Now our mother is going to sleep,
        Going to sleep.

From our childhood in beauty before us,
  On Jesus, her guide and her stay,
She has leaned : and with calm eyes uplifted,
  She gave Him her hand night and day,
      Night and day.

And while walking in dread and in darkness,
  Through the valley of fears and alarms,
He encouraged her tottering footsteps,
  And now she falls into His arms,
      Into His arms.

She hears His dear voice in the darkness,
  Oh ! let us all thankfully weep ;
He has called her His " child," His " beloved,"
  And now she has gone to sleep,
      Gone to sleep.

THE OTHER SHORE.

WHAT is it like—that other shore?
  Straining my eyes, I can but see
Skies and ocean that evermore
  Embrace and hide the Beyond from me.
Vainly I wish that an echoed note
  Of the song they sing on the other side,
Over the waters to me may float,
  As I wistfully listen and turn aside.

My Father's house that I have not seen!
  Little I care what its beauties are—
Whether its fields are always green,
  Or the hills are golden that gleam afar;—
Only I know One waiteth there
  Whom my eyes have wearied long to see;
And the country must needs be wondrous fair
  Where Christ the Lord shall welcome me.

What can I do, but watch all day
  Ripples that lazily lap the shore,
The unconscious children at their play,
  While I sit waiting forevermore?
Waiting still at the water-side—
  When will the boatman come for me,
And bear me off on the flowing tide
  To land where my best belovèd be?

Nay, but my Father for me will send,
  When I have finished the task He gave;
When I have proved me His child and friend
  By the Christ-like spirit, meek, yet brave.
Why should I list to the waves' sad sighs,
  Dreamily waiting for what delays?
Let me rather with strength arise,
  And work for Him the remaining days.

"BABES ALWAYS."

'TIS late—in my lone chamber,
   Borne through the echoing hall,
I hear the wind's hoarse sobbing,
   The rain-drops' plashing fall;
And the street-lamp, on the ceiling,
   Throws many a weird-like form—
Tree-shadows, dancing wildly
   To the music of the storm.

Called I my vigil lonely?
   The door is still and fast;
O'er threshold and o'er carpet
   No mortal foot has passed;
No rustle of white raiment
   Or warm breath stirs the air;
Yet I speak aloud my greeting—
   "My darlings! are you there?"

Not the three who, by me kneeling,
   Said, "Our Father," hours ago;
Whose cheeks now dent their pillows—
   Live roses upon snow.
They dream not of the graveyard
   And of the hillocks twain,
Snow-heaped to-night (Lord, help me!)
   And dripping with the rain!

"BABES ALWAYS."

Twelve years!—a manly stripling,
    Our boy, by this had grown!
Is it four years, or twenty,
    Since I kissed the eyelids down
Of her whose baby-sweetness
    Was a later gift from God,
And straightened in the coffin
    Wee feet that never trod?

These are not strangers' glances
    That eagerly seek mine;
I know the loving straining
    Of the arms that round me twine.
Thou hast kept them babes, O Father!
    Who, not 'mid Heaven's bowers,
Learning the speech of angels,
    Forget this home of ours;

Or her, who braved Death's anguish
    To win them to her breast,
If they fled into the sunshine—
    Free birds from narrow nest—
They come to me when longing
    And pain are at their height,
To tell me of the safety,
    The love and the delight

Of that eternal dwelling,
    (With *our* name upon the door!)

The ring of baby-voices
  Shall gladden evermore;
Till, 'neath their tender soothing,
  I lift my heart and smile,
And gather faith and courage
  To bide my " little while."

"I SHALL DIE ALONE."

WHEN the rich gold and purple of Life's sunset
  Lies in its beauty on the silent sea;
When on the shore I see the white-robed angel
  And hear his whisper, " God has called for thee,"—

Eyes lit with love will watch me on the sea-shore,
  Warm human hands will fondly press my own;
But can I bear them with me on my journey
  Out through the dimness of the world unknown?

And this great beauty of the earth and heavens,
  The holy night whose glory fills my soul,
The softened amethyst of fading twilight,
  The gleaming stars on night's emblazoned scroll,

The rosy light of morning on the mountains,
  The tender purple of the distant sea—
Things I love now, from henceforth all for-
      gotten ;
  What of their beauty can I bear with me ?

" Alone, alone," sighed gentle-hearted Pascal,
  And yet I think that not alone we die ;
Though all this earth is dimly fading from us,
  Are we alone if one kind Friend is nigh ?

One who hath said, " Lo, I am with you always,"
  The way-worn Man who sat by Galilee,
Speaking good words and healing all the people,
  Who lived and died for love of you and me.

O, not alone, for this our Friend and Brother,
  Though Heaven's great angels bow before
      His throne,
Shall stand with us upon the silent sea-shore,
  His hand shall guide us to the world unknown.

THE NIGHT-WATCH.

" My meditation of Him shall be sweet."—Ps. civ. 34.

O MEDITATION sweet that makes
    The midnight-watch an hour of rest,
And brings, when fickle sleep forsakes,
    A holier calm to hearts oppressed !

THE NIGHT-WATCH.

Soft-speaking as to one so near
   That, kneeling, we might kiss his feet,
The Name above all names most dear,
   Our erst-complaining lips repeat.

Our griefs that Christ alone can guess,
   Our doubts that Christ alone can know,
Flow out to meet His tenderness,
   In tearful confidences flow:

For He who bore all·sorrow, weighed,
   Nailed to His own each lesser cross;
He knows the burden on us laid,
   The secret pain, the hidden loss.

Touched with our woes, He lifteth up
   The humblest follower in His train;
He maketh sweet the bitter cup,
   And death itself is blessèd gain.

Thus, in the lonely night, we learn
   To trust Him most as joys decrease,
And, when our need is sorest, turn
   To hear His silence whisper, *Peace!*

LONGING FOR CHRIST.

MY spirit longs for Thee
   Within my troubled breast,
Although I am unworthy
   Of so Divine a Guest.

Of so Divine a Guest
   Unworthy though I be,
Yet has my heart no rest
   Unless it comes from Thee.

Unless it comes from Thee,
   In vain I look around;
In all that I can see
   No rest is to be found.

No rest is to be found
   But in Thy blessèd love;
O let my wish be crowned,
   And send it from above.

"THOUGH I BE NOTHING."

2 Cor. xii. 11.

MY Father, can I learn so hard a task?
   "You must: no more, my child, of
      you I ask,
Than He hath done—
My well-beloved Son."

"THOUGH I BE NOTHING."

Must I be nothing? Must I nothing do?
"Nothing, my child; Christ hath done all for you.
You cannot buy,
The price is far too high.
Freely I give;
Only 'believe and live.'"

Enough—give Thou the humble heart, and I consent;
Oh! make me nothing, and therewith content.
My gain is loss,
My trust is in the Cross;
Hold me—I'm weak, I fall;
Be Thou mine All in All.

Here give me, Lord, some quiet place
Where I can work, and yet behold Thy face;
While Thou would'st have me stay,
Keep my feet steadfast in Thy way;
They must not tire,
Till Thou shalt bid me "Come up higher."

I will be nothing still,
That Christ alone my heaven of heavens may fill.
Yet set me, Lord, a little, glowing gem
Upon His diadem;
To shed my tiny ray
Among the splendors of His crowning day;
Though unperceived, I still should like to shine,
A tribute-glory on that brow divine.

And let me raise
One little note of praise,
Though scarcely heard among the myriad voices,
When the redeemed Church above rejoices;
That it may blend
With angel hallelujahs that ascend,
A lowly offering to my Saviour-Friend.
Lord, I am nothing! Christ in all must shine:
Do with me as thou wilt, for I am Thine.

HYMN OF REST.

COME, all ye weary, worn, and sin-defiled,
    The day of whose deliverance hath not
        smiled—
Who toil on, sorrow-laden, sore distressed,
Come unto Me, and I will give you rest!

Come, ye who seek, through all the world of sin,
The precious treasure only found within;
Clasp your eternal jewel of the breast,
Come unto Me, and I will give you rest!

Come, ye for whom the human love hath proved
A longing to be infinitely loved,
Whose hearts yet hover round some empty nest,
Come unto Me, and I will give you rest!

Come, ye who suffer through the lone, long
    night,
And grope for day with sad, tear-blinded sight;
I am the sun that sets not in the west,
I bring you healing, and will bring you rest!

Come, all who bear the cross where I have trod;
Who climb the same ascent to get to God,
Bowed down to see the prints My feet have
    pressed,
Come unto me, and I will give you rest!

When the storms rise, and seas of trouble roll,
I will be near to save the sinking soul;
Each wave that breaks shall lift, dilate your
    breast,
And in their motion—I will give you rest!

"IF GOD SHALL BLESS ME SO."

IN years long past, I said, "If God shall give
    Me certain blessings;—cause my path to
    lead
Through ways of comfort—grant me long to
    live,
  And strength sufficient for life's utmost need,
Much joy shall surely through these channels
    flow;
    If God shall bless me so.

Friends, and fair honors, should He grant me
    these,
  Home-love, and children, and some skill to
    grasp
From the rich world its opportunities—
  What more could heart desire, or full hands
    clasp?
Surely my life like some glad tune shall go,
    If God shall bless me so.

But now I say, "If God shall grant me heaven;"
  And so end there. If I at length shall come
Into His presence who Himself hath given,
  All better gifts must lie in that vast sum.
No good thing there shall be withheld, I know,
    If God shall bless me so.

HYMN OF FAITH.

TOSSING at night upon a stormy sea,
  What earthly help can now avail for thee?
How the frail boat, on which thy hopes are cast,
Shivers and trembles in the rising blast.

Lift up thine eyes! Behold! upon the wave,
  The Lord draws near, thy trembling life to
    save.
He knows thy peril, though thy lips are dumb;
Across the watery waste He bids thee come.

Cling to no frail supports that round thee float;
Arise, and quickly leave thy sinking boat:
Strong in His strength, and in His courage
    brave,
Stand thou upright upon the slippery wave.

Think not how high the angry waters rise;
Think not that men will gaze with wondering
    eyes;
Think not it is thine own exalted power
Upholds thy feet upon that treacherous floor.

But fix thine eye upon that face divine;
Take the kind hand so gladly stretched for
    thine;
Let not thy clear faith waver nor grow dim:
So on the water shalt thou walk to Him.

THE LATTICE AT SUNRISE.

AS on my bed at dawn I mused and prayed,
    I saw my lattice prankt upon the wall,
  The flaunting leaves and flitting birds withal:
A sunny phantom interlaced with shade;
"Thanks be to heaven," in happy mood I said,
  "What sweeter aid my matins could befall
Than this fair glory from the East hath made?
  What holy sleights hath God the Lord of all,

To bid us feel and see? We are not free
   To say we see not, for the glory comes
Nightly and daily, like the flowing sea;
   His lustre pierceth through the midnight
      glooms;
And at prime hour, behold! He follows me
   With golden shadows to my secret rooms!"

GOOD-BYE.

GOOD-BYE, good-bye, it is the sweetest
      blessing
That falls from mortal lips on mortal ear,
The weakness of our human love confessing,
   The promise that a love more strong is near—
      May God be with you!

Why do we say it when the tears are starting?
   Why must a word so sweet bring only pain?
Our love seems all-sufficient till the parting,
   And then we feel it impotent and vain—
      May God be with you!

Oh, may He guide, and bless, and keep you
      ever,
   He who is strong to battle with your foes;
Whoever fails, His love can fail you never,
   And all you need He in His wisdom knows—
      May God be with you!

Better than earthly presence, e'en the dearest,
  Is the great blessing that our partings bring;
For in the loneliest moments God is nearest,
  And from our sorrows heavenly comforts spring,
    If God be with us.

Good-bye, good-bye, with latest breath we say it,
  A legacy of hope, and faith, and love;
Parting must come, we cannot long delay it,
  But, one in Him, we hope to meet above,
    If God be with us.

Good-bye—'tis all we have for one another;
  Our love, more strong than death, is helpless still,
For none can take the burden from his brother,
  Or shield, except by prayer, from any ill—
    May God be with you!

I AM HIS AND HE IS MINE.

LONG did I toil, and knew no earthly rest;
  Far did I rove, and found no certain home;
At last I sought them in His shelt'ring breast,
  Who spreads His arms and bids the weary come.

I AM HIS AND HE IS MINE.

With Him I found a home, a rest divine;
And I since then am His and He is mine.

Yes, He is mine! and naught of earthly things,
  Not all the charms of pleasure, wealth, or power,
The fame of heroes, or the pomp of kings,
  Could tempt me to forego His love an hour.
"Go, worthless world," I cry, "with all that's thine;
Go! I my Saviour's am, and He is mine."

The good I have is from His store supplied;
  The ill is only what He deems the best;
With Him my Friend, I'm rich with naught beside,
  And poor without Him, though of all possessed.
Changes may come—I take or I resign—
Content while I am His and He is mine.

Whate'er may change, in Him no change is seen:
  A glorious Sun that wanes not nor declines;
Above the clouds and storms He walks serene,
  And sweetly on His people's darkness shines.
All may depart—I fret not, nor repine,
While I my Saviour's am, and He is mine.

He stays me falling; lifts me up when down;
   Reclaims me wandering; guards from every
      foe;
Plants on my worthless brow the victor's crown,
   Which, in return, before His feet I throw,
Grieved that I cannot better grace His shrine,
Who deigns to own me His, as He is mine.

While here, alas! I know but half His love,
   But half discern Him, and but half adore;
But when I meet Him in the realms above,
   I hope to love Him better, praise Him more,
And feel and tell, amid the choir divine,
How fully I am His and He is mine.

TIRED MOTHERS.

A LITTLE elbow leans upon your knee—
   Your tired knee that has so much to
      bear;
A child's dear eyes are looking lovingly
   From underneath a thatch of tangled hair.
Perhaps you do not heed the velvet touch
   Of warm, moist fingers, folding yours so
      tight;
You do not prize this blessing overmuch—
   You almost are too tired to pray to-night.

But it is a blessedness. A year ago
    I did not see it as I do to-day—
We are so dull and thankless, and too slow
    To catch the sunshine till it slips away.
And now it seems surpassing strange to me
    That, while I wore the badge of motherhood,
I did not kiss more oft and tenderly
    The little child that brought me only good.

And if, some night, when you sit down to rest,
    You miss this elbow from your tired knee,
This restless, curling head from off your breast,
    This lisping tongue that chatters constantly;
If from your own the dimpled hands had slipped,
    And ne'er would nestle in your palm again;
If the white feet into the grave had tripped,
    I could not blame you for your heartache then.

I wonder so that mothers ever fret
    At little children clinging to their gown;
Or that the footprints, when the days are wet,
    Are ever black enough to make them frown.
If I could find a little muddy boot,
    Or cap, or jacket on my chamber floor;
If I could kiss a rosy, restless foot,
    And hear its patter in my home once more.

If I could mend a broken cart to-day,
    To-morrow make a kite to reach the sky—

There is no woman in God's world could say
  She was more blissfully content than I.
But ah! the dainty pillow next my own
  Is never rumpled by a shining head;
My singing birdling from its nest is flown;
  The little boy I used to kiss is dead.

BEST.

MOTHER, I see you with your nursery light,
Leading your babies, all in white,
      To their sweet rest:
Christ, the Good Shepherd, carries *mine* to-night,
      And that is best!

I cannot help tears, when I see them twine
Their fingers in yours, and their bright curls shine
      On your warm breast;
But the Saviour's is purer than yours or mine—
      He can love best!

You tremble each hour because your arms
Are weak; your heart is wrung with alarms,
      And sore opprest;
My darlings are safe, out of reach of harms,
      And that is best!

You know over yours may hang even now
Pain and disease, whose fulfilling slow
   Naught can arrest;
Mine in God's gardens run to and fro,
   And that is best!

You know that of yours the feeblest one
And dearest, may live long years alone,
   Unloved, unblest;
Mine are cherished of saints around God's throne,
   And that is best!

You must dread for yours the crime that sears,
Dark guilt unwashed by repentant tears,
   And unconfessed;
Mine entered spotless on eternal years.
   Oh, how *much* the best!

But grief is selfish, and I cannot see
Always why I should so stricken be,
   More than the rest;
But I know that, as well as for them, for *me*
   God did the best!

"IT IS I; BE NOT AFRAID."

"And He said, Come."

LORD, it is Thou! and I can walk
   Upon the heaving sea,
Firm in a vexed, unquiet way,
   Because I come to Thee.
If Thou art all I hope to gain,
   And all I fear to miss,
There is a highway for my heart
   Through rougher seas than this.

And step by step on even ground
   My trembling foot shall fall,
Led by Thy calm, inviting voice,
   Thou Lord and Heir of all.
The very thing I cannot bear,
   And have not power to do,
I hail the grace that could prepare
   For me to carry through.

These waters would not hold me up
   If Thou wert not my end;
But whom Thou callest to Thyself
   Even winds and waves defend.
Our very perils shut us in
   To Thy supporting care;
We venture on the awful deep,
   And find our courage there.

Oh, there are heavenly heights to reach
  In many a fearful place,
Where the poor timid heir of God
  Lies blindly on his face;
Lies languishing for life divine
  That he shall never see
Till he go forward at Thy sign,
  And trust himself to Thee.

Forth from some narrow, frail defense,
  Some rest, Thyself below,
Some poor content with less than all,
  My soul is called to go.
Yes, I will come! I will not wait
  An outward calm to see,
And, O my glory, be Thou great
  Even in the midst of me.

WATCH!

Matt. xxiv. 42.

"WATCH! for ye know not the hour,"
  When Christ your Lord shall come;
Come, with tender impatience,
  To take His chosen home;
Home to "the place" He has made them,
  Of beauty untold above;
Home to the house of the Father,
  Home to His glory and love!

"Watch! for ye know not the hour!"
   It may be He stands at the door:
It may be but a moment,
   And your care and sin are o'er;
It may be His hand is lifted,
   Even this moment, to knock;
Are you waiting, are you watching,
   With your hand upon the lock?

"Watch! for ye know not the hour!"
   Suppose that He should come,
And find that you were not watching,
   Or thinking of going home:
With all the house ungarnished,
   And all the lights grown dim;
Suppose He should knock unheeded,
   And no welcome ready for Him!

"Watch! for ye know not the hour!"
   I am waiting, Lord, to catch
The first sound of Thy footfall,
   With my hand upon the latch;
I am waiting, O blessed Jesus,
   For the sound of Thy longed-for knock;
Then, with an eager welcome,
   Quick I shall turn the lock.

O glad, O blessèd hour!
   It draweth on apace,

When my glorious Lord shall enter,
  And I shall " see His face ;"
And well do I remember,
  That He calls those servants blest,
Who are found by their Master watching.
  What words can tell the rest?

'TWILL NOT BE LONG!

'TWILL not be long—this wearying commotion
  That marks its passage in the human breast,
And, like the billows on the heaving ocean,
  That ever rock the cradle of unrest,
Will soon subside ; the happy time is nearing,
  When bliss, not pain, shall have its rich increase ;
E'en unto thee the dove may now be steering
  With gracious message. Wait, and hold thy peace ;
    'Twill not be long !

The lamps go out : the stars give up their shining ;
  The world is lost in darkness for a while ;
And foolish hearts give way to sad repining,
  And feel as though they ne'er again could smile.

Why murmur thus, the needful lesson scorning?
  Oh, read thy Teacher and His word aright.
The world would have no greeting for the morning,
  If 'twere not for the darkness of the night;
    'Twill not be long!

'Twill not be long; the strife will soon be ended;
  The doubts, the fears, the agony, the pain
Will seem but as the clouds that low descended,
  To yield their pleasure to the parchèd plain.
The times of weakness and of sore temptations,
  Of bitter grief and agonizing cry;
These earthly cares and ceaseless tribulations
  Will bring a blissful harvest by and by.
    'Twill not be long!

'Twill not be long; the eye of faith discerning
  The wondrous glory that shall be revealed,
Instructs the soul, that every day is learning
  The better wisdom which the world concealed.
And soon, aye, soon, there'll be an end of teaching,
  When mortal vision finds immortal sight,
And her true place the soul in gladness reaching,
  Beholds the glory of the Infinite.
    'Twill not be long!

"'Twill not be long!" the heart goes on re-
    peating;
  It is the burden of the mourner's song;
The work of grace in us He is completing,
  Who thus assures us—" It will not be long."
His rod and staff our fainting steps sustain-
    ing,
  Our hope and comfort every day will be;
And we may bear our cross as uncomplaining
  As He who leads us unto Calvary.
        'Twill not be long!

HEREAFTER.

NOT from the flowers of earth,
    Not from the stars,
  Not from the voicing sea,
      May we
  The secret wrest which bars
      Our knowledge here,
Of all we hope and all that we may fear
      Hereafter.

  We watch beside our graves,
      Yet meet no sign
  Of where our dear ones dwell.
      Ah! well,

Even now, your dead and mine
    May long to speak
Of raptures it were wiser we should seek
      Hereafter.

Oh, hearts we fondly love!
    Oh, pallid lips
That bore our farewell kiss
    From this
To yonder world's eclipse!
    Do ye, safe home,
Smile at your earthly doubts of what would come
      Hereafter?

Grand birthright of the soul,
    Naught may despoil!
Oh, precious, healing balm,
    To calm
Our lives in pain and toil!
    God's boon, that we
Or soon or late shall know what is to be
      Hereafter.

WRITTEN ON RECOVERY FROM ILLNESS.

"Not my will, but Thine be done."—LUKE xxii. 42.

IT is Thy will, my Lord, my God!
    And I, whose feet so lately trod
  The margin of the tomb,

ON RECOVERY FROM ILLNESS.

Must now retrace my weary way,
And in this land of exile stay,
   Far from my heavenly home.

It is Thy will;—and this, to me,
A check to every thought shall be,
   Which else might dare rebel;
Those sacred words contain a balm,
Each sad regret to soothe and calm,
   Each murmuring thought to quell.

It is Thy will;—that will be done!
To Thee the fittest time is known,
   When, by Thy grace made meet,
My longing soul shall soar away,
And leave her prison-house of clay,
   To worship at Thy feet.

It is Thy will;—and must be mine,
Though here, far off from Thee, I pine,
   And find no place of rest;
When shall the poor bewildered dove,
Now o'er the waters doomed to rove,
   Be sheltered in Thy breast?

It is Thy will;—and now anew
Let me my earthly path pursue,
   With one determined aim—

To Thee, to consecrate each power,
To Thee, to dedicate each hour,
  And glorify Thy name.

It is Thy will ;—I seek no more :
Yet, if I cast towards that bright shore,
  A longing, tearful eye,
It is because, when landed there,
Sin will no more my heart ensnare,
  Nor Satan e'er draw nigh.

THE HARDEST TIME OF ALL.

THERE are days of deepest sorrow
  In the season of our life ;
There are wild, despairing moments,
  There are hours of mental strife,
There are times of stony anguish,
  When the tears refuse to fall ;
But the waiting time, my brothers,
  Is the hardest time of all.

Youth and love are oft impatient,
  Seeking things beyond their reach ;
And the heart grows sick with hoping,
  Ere it learns what life can teach.
For, before the fruit be gathered,
  We must see the blossoms fall ;
And the waiting time, my brothers,
  Is the hardest time of all.

THE HARDEST TIME OF ALL.

Loving once, and loving ever,
   It is sad to watch for years
For the light whose fitful shining
   Makes a rainbow of our tears.
It is sad to count at morning
   All the hours to evenfall;
Oh, the waiting time, my brothers,
   Is the hardest time of all!

We can bear the heat of conflict,
   Though the sudden crushing blow,
Beating back our gathered forces,
   For a moment lay us low.
We may rise again beneath it,
   None the weaker for our fall;
But the waiting time, my brothers,
   Is the hardest time of all.

For it wears the eager spirit,
   As the salt waves wear the stone,
And Hope's gorgeous garb grows threadbare,
   Till its brightest tints are gone.
Then, amid youth's radiant tresses,
   Silent snows begin to fall;
Oh, the waiting time, my brothers,
   Is the hardest time of all!

Yet at last we learn the lesson,
   That God knoweth what is best,

And a silent resignation
  Makes the spirit calm and blest;
For, perchance, a day is coming,
  For the changes of our fate,
When our hearts will thank Him meekly
  That He taught us how to wait.

"FOLLOW ME."

THE Master's voice was sweet—
  "I give My life for thee;
Bear thou this cross through pain and loss,
  Arise and follow Me."
I clasped it in my hands,—
  O Thou that died for me,
The day is bright, my step is light,
  'Tis sweet to follow Thee.

Through the long summer day
  I followed lovingly;
'Twas bliss to hear *His* voice so near,
  His glorious face to see.
Down where the lilies pale
  Fringed the bright river's brim,
In pastures green, His steps were seen;
  'Twas sweet to follow Him.

Oh, sweet to follow Him!
  "Lord, let us here abide."

"FOLLOW ME."

The flowers were fair, I lingered there,
   I laid His cross aside.
I saw His face no more
   By that bright river's brim;
Before me lay the desert way,
   'Twas hard to follow Him.

Yes, hard to follow Him
   Into that dreary land;
I was alone—His cross had grown
   Too heavy for my hand.
I heard His voice afar
   Sound through the night air chill;
My tired feet refused to meet
   His coming o'er the hill.

My Master's voice was sad—
   "I gave My life for thee,
I bore the cross through pain and loss,
   Thou hast not followed Me."
So fair the lilied banks,
   So bleak the desert way—
The night was dark, I could not mark
   Where Thy blest footsteps lay.

Fairer the lilied banks,
   Softer the glassy lea,
The *endless* rest of them who best
   Have learned to follow Me.

Canst thou not follow Me,
    All weary as thou art?
Hath patient love no power to move
    Thy slow and faithless heart?
Wilt thou not follow Me?
    These weary feet of Mine
Have stained red the pathway dread,
    In searching for thee and thine.

O Lord! O Love Divine!
    Once more I follow Thee;
Let me abide so near Thy side,
    That I Thy face may see.
I clasp Thy piercèd hand,
    Oh, Thou that died for me!
I'll bear Thy cross through pain and loss,
    So I may cling to Thee.

PEACE.

IS this the peace of God, this strange, sweet calm?
    The weary day is at its zenith still,
    Yet 'tis as if beside some cool clear rill,
Through shadowy stillness rose an evening psalm,
And all the noise of life were hushed away,
And tranquil gladness reigned with gently soothing sway.

It was not so just now. I turned aside
　　With aching head, and heart most sorely
　　　　bowed;
　　Around me cares and griefs in crushing
　　　　crowd;
While inly rose the sense, in swelling tide,
Of weakness, insufficiency, and sin, -
And fear, and gloom, and doubt in mighty
　　　　flood rolled in.

That rushing flood I had no power to meet,
　　Nor strength to flee: my present future past,
　　My self, my sorrow, and my sin, I cast
In utter helplessness at Jesus' feet;
Then bent before the storm, if such His will.
He saw the winds and waves, and whispered,
　　　　"Peace, be still!"

And there was calm! O Saviour, I have proved
　　That Thou to help and save art *truly* near;
　　How else this quiet rest from grief and fear,
And all distress? The cross is not removed,
I must go forth to bear it as before,
But leaning on Thine arm, I dread its weight
　　　　no more.

Is it, indeed, Thy peace? I have not tried
　　To analyze my faith, dissect my trust,
　　Or measure if belief be full and just,

And, *therefore*, claim Thy peace. But Thou
    hast died.
I know that this is true, and true for me,
And, knowing it, I come, and cast my all on
    Thee.

It is not that I feel less weak, but Thou
    Wilt be my strength ; it is not that I see
    Less sin ; but more of pardoning love in
        Thee,
And all-sufficient grace. Enough ! And now
All fluttering thought is stilled ; I only rest,
And feel that Thou art near, and know that I
    am blessed.

A HYMN

I CANNOT think but God must know
    About the thing I long for so ;
I know He is so good, so kind,
I cannot think but He will find
Some way to help, some way to show
Me to the thing I long for so.

I stretch my hand—it lies so near :
It looks so sweet, it looks so dear.
"Dear Lord," I pray, " Oh, let me know
If it is wrong to want it so ? "

He only smiles—He does not speak:
My heart grows weaker and more weak,
With looking at the thing so dear,
Which lies so far, and yet so near.

Now, Lord, I leave at Thy loved feet
This thing which looks so near, so sweet;
I will not seek, I will not long—
I almost fear I have been wrong.
I'll go and work the harder, Lord,
And wait till by some loud, clear word
Thou callest me to Thy loved feet,
To take this thing so dear, so sweet.

NONE OR ALL.

"LORD, I will follow Thee," I said,
    "And give to Thee my heart,
And for the world and self will keep
    Only a little part;
A little part what time my soul
    Grows weary, worn, and sad,
A little spot where earthly joys
    May come to make me glad."
But on my ear it seemed to me,
    I heard a whisper fall:
"I cannot halve thy heart with thee;
    Give none to Me—or all."

NONE OR ALL.

"But, Lord, the world is fair," I said,
  "I would not go astray,
Yet sometimes may I pluck a flower
  Outside the narrow way?
Yet sometimes may I sit serene,
  Nor spirit-conflicts share,
Just shifting for a space, the cross
  I am content to bear?"
Yet once again it seemed to me
  I heard the whisper fall:
"I cannot halve thy heart with thee;
  Give none to Me—or all."

"Ah, Lord, my every hope," I said,
  "On Thee my soul doth rest,
And I am sure the very way
  Thou leadest me is best;
And if I've thought too straight the path,
  Too stern the hindering vows,
Teach me that naught of real bliss
  Thy service disallows."
More softly still it seemed to me,
  I heard the whisper fall:
"I will not halve My Heaven with thee,
  Then give to Me thine all!"

WANDERING.

I HAVE wandered to the mountain,
    And the night is dark and cold;
I am lost! O Heavenly Shepherd,
    Where is the Fold?

I am weary, I am helpless,
    But still hoping as I stand,
Reaching out into the darkness,
    To feel Thy hand.

I am looking for Thy coming,
    For the Fold and safety there—
I shall perish, loving Shepherd,
    Without Thy care.

Hark! I hear the Shepherd calling,
    And the morning sky of gold
Sends a light across the mountain—
    I see the Fold!

THE LAST HOUR.

IF I were told that I must die to-morrow,
    That the next sun
Which sinks, should bear me past all fear and sorrow
    For any one,
All the fight fought, all the short journey through,
    What should I do?

I do not think that I should shrink or falter,
    But just go on,
Doing my work, nor change, nor seek to alter
    Aught that is gone;
But rise, and move, and love, and smile, and pray
    For one more day.

And, lying down at night for a last sleeping,
    Say in that ear
Which hearkens ever: "Lord, within Thy keeping,
    How should I fear?
And, when to-morrow brings Thee nearer still,
    Do Thou Thy will."

I might not sleep for awe; but peaceful, tender,
    My soul would lie

All the night long; and when the morning
    splendor
        Flushed o'er the sky,
I think that I could smile—could calmly say,
        " It is His day."

But if a wondrous hand from the blue, yonder,
        Held out a scroll,
On which my life was writ, and I with wonder
        Beheld unroll
To a long century's end its mystic clue,
        What should I do?

What *could* I do, O blessed Guide and Master?
        Other than this:
Still to go on as now, not slower, faster,
        Nor fear to miss
The road, although so very long it be,
        While led by Thee?

Step after step, feeling Thee close beside me,
        Although unseen,
Through thorns, through flowers, whether the
    tempest hide Thee,
        Or heavens serene,
Assured Thy faithfulness cannot betray,
        Thy love decay.

I may not know, my God, no hand revealeth
        Thy counsels wise;

Along the path a deepening shadow stealeth,
    No voice replies
To all my questioning thought, the time to tell,
    And it is well.

Let me keep on, abiding and unfearing
    Thy will always,
Through a long century's ripening fruition,
    Or a short day's,
Thou can'st not come too soon; and I can wait,
    If Thou come late.

PRAY WITHOUT CEASING.

"Pray without ceasing," says the zealous Paul;
  But what means this? Must we not work, nor eat,
Nor take our rest? Is prayer to swallow all?
  Are knees to serve in lieu of hands and feet?
Nay, I will show thee what is ceaseless prayer.
First, 'tis a heart to prayer for aye inclined;
  Next, that it be of all our choicest care;
  Next, that we ask the Counselor to share
Each sorrow of the body and the mind;
Next, that we cease not till our good we find,
  Like him who said, "I will not let thee part
  Until thou bless;" next, that our spirits dart

Their pious glances, when they can, on high;
Last, that we bound each day with morn and
    evening cry.

TRANSVERSE AND PARALLEL.

MY will, dear Lord, from Thine doth run
    Too oft a different way;
'Tis hard to say, " Thy will be done,"
    In every darkened day!
        My heart grows chill
        To see Thy will
Turn all life's gold to gray.

My will is set to gather flowers,
    Thine blights them in my hand;
Mine reaches for life's sunny hours,
    Thine leads through shadow-land;
        And all my days
        Go on in ways
I cannot understand.

Yet more and more this truth doth shine
    From failure and from loss,
The will that runs transverse to Thine
    Doth thereby make its cross:
        Thine upright will
        Cuts straight and still
Through pride, and dream, and dross.

But if in parallel to Thine
  My will doth meekly run,
All things in heaven and earth are mine,
  My will is crossed by none :
    Thou art in me,
    And I in Thee—
Thy will—and mine—are done !

"*JESUS, HELP CONQUER!*"

JESUS, help conquer !
    My spirit is sinking,
Deep waters of sorrow go over my head ;
    Weeping and trembling,
    And fearing and shrinking,
I watch for the day, and night cometh instead :
    Bitter the cup
    I am hourly drinking ;
How thorny the path that I hourly tread !

    Jesus, help conquer !
    For, fainting and weary,
Scarcely my hands can their weapons sustain ;
    The way seems so desolate,
    Painful and dreary,
How shall I ever to heaven attain ?
    Jesus, great Captain !
    If Thou be not near me,
How shall I ever the victory gain ?

"JESUS, HELP CONQUER!"

Jesus, help conquer!
Earth holds out her lure,
And mortal affections yearn after the prize:
　　Scarcely my heart
　　Can the struggle endure;
Scarce can I lift up my tear-blinded eyes.
　　Jesus! Redeemer!
　　The promise is sure;
Speak to my spirit and bid me arise.

Jesus, help conquer!
There is not an hour
Of sorrow, or joy, but is ordered by Thee;
　　Thou dost cut down
　　Who hast planted the flower—
Tempest or calm at Thy bidding shall be:
　　Look on my sorrow,
　　And give me the power
Humbly to wait till Thou comfortest me.

Jesus, help conquer!
Lord, turn not away:
See with what power the billows increase!
　　Give me Thy love
　　For my comfort and stay!
Then shall my trembling and murmuring cease;
　　Then shall my spirit
　　Grow strong for the fray—
Then shall this weary heart rest in Thy peace.

Jesus, help conquer!
I cry unto Thee;
Hardly my heart its petitions can frame,
All is so dark
And so painful to me.
All I can utter sometimes is Thy Name:
Jesus, help conquer!
My portion now be;
Though all else should change, be Thou ever
the same!

THE COMING.

I GATHERED flowers the summer long:
I dozed the days on sunny leas,
And wove my fancies into song,
Or dreamed in aimless ease.

Or watched, from jutting cliffs, the dyes
Of changeful waters under me—
The lazy gulls that dip and rise,
White specks upon the sea:

And far away, where blue to blue
Was wed, the ships that came and went;
And thought, O happy world! and drew
Therefrom a full content.

THE COMING.

My mates toiled in the ripening field,
    Nor paused for rest in cool or heat;
The yellow grain made haste to yield
    Its harvesting complete:

My mates toiled in their pleasant homes,
    They plucked the fruit from laden boughs,
And sang, "For if the Master comes
    And find no ready house!"

And far and strange their singing seemed,
    And harsh the voices every one,
That woke the pleasant dream I dream'd
    To thought of tasks undone.

Yet still I waited, lingered still,
    Won by a cloud—a soaring lark;
Till by and by, the land was chill,
    And all the sky was dark.

And lo! the Master! through the night
    My mates come forth to welcome Him:
Their labor done, their garments white,
    While mine are stained and dim.

They bring to Him their golden sheaves;
    To Him their finished toil belongs;
While I have but these withered leaves,
    And these poor, foolish songs!

HOPE'S SONG.

I HEAR it singing, singing sweetly,
   Softly in an undertone,
Singing as if God had taught it,
   "It is better farther on!"

Night and day it sings the sonnet,
   Sings it while I sit alone,
Sings it so my heart will hear it,
   "It is better farther on!"

Sits upon the grave and sings it,
   Sings it when the heart would groan,
Sings it when the shadows darken,
   "It is better farther on!"

Farther on! How much farther?
   Count the mile-stones one by one.
No; no counting—only trusting
   "It is better farther on!"

THE PETRIFIED FERN.

IN a valley, centuries ago,
   Grew a little fern leaf, green and slender,
  Veining delicate, and fibres tender;
Waving when the wind crept down so low;

THE PETRIFIED FERN.

Rushes tall, and moss, and grass grew round it,
Playful sunbeams darted in and found it,
Drops of dew stole in, by night, and crowned it,
But no foot of man e'er trod that way,
Earth was young and keeping holiday.

Monster fishes swam the silent main,
Stately forests waved their giant branches,
Mountains hurled their snowy avalanches,
Mammoth creatures stalked across the plain;
Nature reveled in grand mysteries;
But the little fern was not of these,—
Did not number with the hills and trees,
Only grew and waved its wild sweet way;
None came to note it day by day.

Earth, one time, put on a frolic mood,
Heaved the rocks and changed the mighty motion
Of the deep, strong currents of the ocean;
Moved the plain, and shook the haughty wood,
Crushed the little fern in soft, moist clay,
Covered it, and hid it safe away.
Oh, the long, long centuries since that day!
Oh, the agony! oh, life's bitter cost!
Since that useless little fern was lost!

Useless! Lost! There came a thoughtful man
   Searching Nature's secrets, far and deep;
   From a fissure in a rocky steep
He withdrew a stone, o'er which there ran
   Fairy pencilings, a quaint design,
   Veinings, leafage, fibres clear and fine,
   And the fern's life lay in every line!
So, I think, God hides some souls away,
Sweetly to surprise us, the last day.

LOOKING SEAWARD.

THE fretted waters of the bay
   Roll golden in the rising sun,
And swiftly o'er the shining way
   The ships go gliding one by one.

Athwart the hills that grandly lie,
   Dipping their bare feet in the sea,
The sails, like white clouds floating by,
   Cast quaint, quick shadows as they flee.

Far out, where sky and ocean run
   To one bright line of light and foam,
Those motes that glisten in the sun
   Are happy vessels bounding home.

And here, amid the city, whirled
   By toil, and strife, and care, we stand

And look upon that ocean world,
    As souls look on the promised land.

Here, all things weary seem, and worn;
    Our eyes are stained with dust and tears;
But there, whence those bright motes are borne,
    How pure and lovely earth appears!

'Tis so; for now, were we with those
    Whose eyes have, sure, a longing gleam,
On the far-coming ships, who knows,
    How precious might this haven seem?

What storms and perils hardly passed—
    What days of doubt and nights of fear—
Have strained the hearts that now, at last,
    Draw nearer home, and still more near!

This is a type of all our days;
    Forever holding up the glass
To gaze far-off through golden rays
    On things whereto we may not pass.

Forever thinking joys that are,
    Are sodden, dull, and full of pain;
And those that glisten from afar
    Hold all the gloss and all the gain!

A SONG IN THE NIGHT.

"When I awake, I am still with Thee."—PSALM cxxxix. 18.

IN silence of the middle night,
   I awake to be with Thee;
And through the shadows as the light
   Thy mercy smiles on me.

I talk with Thee upon my bed,
   In meditation blest,
And sweetly pillow there my head,
   Upon my Saviour's breast.

I think of Him who knelt and prayed
   At midnight on the hill;
Then walked the sea, His friends to aid,
   And bid the storm be still.

I think of Him who took the cup,
   In dark Gethsemane,
And gathering strength from prayer rose up
   To die for such as me.

I think of heaven, where never more
   The weary ask for night,
But ever fresh'ning glories pour
   New raptures on the sight.

ASPIRATION.

So do I learn a parable
  That in my darkest day,
When waves of sorrow round me swell,
  The storm shall pass away.

Nor will I turn my head aside,
  Though bitter griefs be mine;
But say with Him, the Crucified—
  Father, my will is Thine.

Thus shall I praise Thee while I've breath,
  To sing Thy love to me,
And welcome e'en the night of death,
  To wake and be with Thee.

ASPIRATION.

TAKE the praise we bring Thee, Lord,
  Something more than what we speak,
For the love within us feels
  Words uncertain, cold, and weak—
Thoughts that rise and tears that fall,
Praise Thee better: take them all!

Looking back the way we've come,
  What a sight, O Lord, we see!
All the failure in ourselves,
  All the love and strength in Thee.

Yet it seemed so dark before—
Would that we had trusted more!

We will shun no future storm,
   Sure Thy voice is in its wind;
We'll confront each coming cloud,
   Sure the sun is bright behind:
Praying then, or praising now,
Only wilt Thou teach us how!

When at last the end shall come,
   What, O Lord, is Death but this,
Door of our dear Father's home,
   Entrance into perfect bliss,
Peril past and labor done,
Sorrow over, peace begun?

IF I SHOULD DIE TO-NIGHT.

IF I should die to-night,
  My friends would look upon my quiet face
Before they laid it in its resting-place,
And deem that death had left it almost fair;
And laying snow-white flowers against my hair,
Would smooth it down with careful tenderness,
And fold my hands with lingering caress—
  Poor hands, so empty and so cold to-night!

IF I SHOULD DIE TO-NIGHT.

If I should die to-night,
My friends would call to mind, with loving thought,
Some kindly deed the icy hands had wrought;
Some gentle word the frozen lips had said;
Errands on which the willing feet had sped;
The memory of my selfishness and pride,
My hasty words, would all be put aside,
And so I should be loved and mourned to-night!

If I should die to-night,
Even hearts estranged would turn once more to me,
Recalling other days remorsefully;
The eyes that chill me with averted glance
Would look upon me as of yore, perchance,
And soften in the old, familiar way,
For who could war with dumb, unconscious clay?
So I might rest, forgiven of all, to-night!

Oh, friends! I pray to-night,
Keep not your kisses for my dead, cold brow—
The way is lonely; let me feel them now.
Think gently of me; I am travel-worn,
My faltering feet are pierced with many a thorn.
Forgive, O hearts estranged! forgive, I plead!
When dreamless rest is mine I shall not need,
The tenderness for which I longed to-night!

ONE YEAR MORE.

THOU in whose garden I have grown apace,
    Plant of no grace,
    Filling a good tree's place,
Spreading no shade, nor showing any fruit—
Thankless from crown to root!

Thou who, these twenty years, hast come and found
    On tree or ground,
    Sound, be it, or unsound,
No fruit to praise Thee for Thy patient care—
Stubborn, and hard, and bare!

One year more, Master!—one year for my own!
    Let him alone;
    With shame, and sob, and groan,
I'll dig around his heart-roots—graft and prune;
Then, if, for all, he bear not!—ah! so soon?
    Ah! give me *one year more!*

I THIRST.

DOWN through the hushed and thickening air,
    And gathering gloom of earth's eclipse,
That weary word, that half-breathed prayer,
    Hath fallen at last from Jesus' lips.

I THIRST.

For three long hours upreared to die,
   For three long hours each sinew straining,
He hath not breathed as yet one sigh
   Could tell of nature's self-complaining.

I thirst! The word is full of pain,
   Of fever-rack, of human anguish,
Of gaping wounds that life-blood drain,
   And leave the heart to faint and languish.

And yet not this, not this alone,
   Hath caused that piteous, sad outburst:
Not human pain hath made that moan,
   Not human want, that mystic thirst.

Thirst to see justice satisfied;
   Thirst to save sinners tempest-tossed;
Thirst to pour out love's boundless tide
   On souls that all unloved were lost;

This was Thy thirst, and this Thy pain,
   This the deep grief Thy bosom nursed:
Say, Jesus, say that word again;
   Still for Thy creatures, Jesus, thirst!

Thirst, that at last our hearts may give
   Torrents of love that thirst to slake;
Thirst, that we too may thirsting live,
   Thirsting to die for Thy sweet sake.

Thirsting to see Thee face to face;
　Thirsting these earthly bonds to sever;
Thirsting for that last, long embrace,
　In which such thirst is quenched forever!

FOR SATURDAY NIGHT.

CHAFED and worn with worldly care,
　Sweetly, Lord, my heart prepare;
Bid this inward tempest cease;
Jesus, come, and whisper peace!
Hush the whirlwind of my will,
With Thyself my spirit fill;
End in calm this busy week,
Let the Sabbath gently break!

Sever, Lord, these earthly ties;
Fain my soul to Thee would rise.
Disentangle me from time,
Lift me to a purer clime,
Let me cast away my load,
Let me now draw nigh to God.
Gently, loving Jesus, speak;
End in calm this busy week.

Draw the curtain of repose
While my weary eyelids close;
Steal my spirit while I rest,
Give me dreamings pure and blest!

Raise me with a cheerful heart;
Holy Ghost, Thyself impart;
Then the Sabbath-day will be
Heaven brought down to earth and me.

A LAY OF PEACE IN SICKNESS.

GOD'S almighty arms are round me—
    Peace, peace is mine!
Judgment scenes need not confound me—
    Peace, peace is mine!
Jesus came Himself and sought me;
Sold to death, He found and bought me,
Then my blessed freedom taught me—
    Peace, peace is mine!

While I hear life's surging billows,
    Peace, peace is mine!
Why suspend my harp on willows?
    Peace, peace is mine!
I may sing with Christ beside me;
Though a thousand ills betide me,
Safely He hath sworn to guide me—
    Peace, peace is mine!

Every trial draws Him nearer—
    Peace, peace is mine!
All His strokes but make Him dearer—
    Peace, peace is mine!

Bless I then the hand that smiteth
Gently, and to heal delighteth;
'Tis against my sins He fighteth—
    Peace, peace is mine!

Welcome every rising sunlight—
    Peace, peace is mine!
Nearer home each rolling midnight—
    Peace, peace is mine!
Death and hell cannot appall me;
Safe in Christ, whate'er befall me,
Calmly wait I till He call me—
    Peace, peace is mine!

TO-DAY!

OH, linger sweet to-day!
    And hasten not away,
Let kindly eyes still shine,
The same old friends be mine,
The joys which, being thine,
    Shall pass with thee away,
    Oh, leave them, kind to-day!

    Oh, hasten, drear to-day!
    Oh, hasten fast away!
For thou sad tears hast brought,
And hours with sorrow fraught,

Fair hopes that came to naught:
   Take, take them all away,
   And linger not to-day!

O infinite to-day,
   That shalt not pass away!
Out of the shadowy night,
Into thy heavenly light,
Under His watchful sight,
   We fain would haste away,
   And call earth yesterday.

NOTHING

O TO be nothing—nothing!
   Only to lie at His feet
A broken, empty vessel,
   Thus for His use made meet!
Emptied, that He may fill me
   As to His service I go,
Broken, so that unhindered
   Through me His life may flow.

O to be nothing—nothing!
   An arrow hid in His hand,
Or a messenger at His gateway
   Waiting for His command;
Only an instrument ready
   For Him to use at His will;

And should He not require me,
  Willing to wait there still.

O to be nothing—nothing!
  Though painful the humbling be;
Though it lay me low in the sight of those
  Who are now, perhaps, praising me;
I would rather be nothing, nothing,
  That to Him be their voices raised,
Who alone is the fountain of blessing,
  Who alone is meet to be praised.

Yet e'en as my pleading rises,
  A voice seems with mine to blend,
And whispers in loving accents,
  "I call thee not servant, but friend.
Fellow-worker with Me I call thee,
  Sharing my sorrows and joy—
Fellow-heir to the glory I have above,
  To treasure without alloy."

Thine may I be, Thine only,
  Till called by Thee to share
The glorious heavenly mansions
  Thou art gone before to prepare.
My heart and soul are yearning
  To see Thee face to face,
With unfettered tongue to praise Thee
  For such heights and depths of grace.

ENTICED.

WITH what clear guile of gracious love enticed,
   I follow forward, as from room to room,
   Through doors that open into light from gloom,
To find and lose, and find again the Christ.

He stands and knocks, and bids me ope the door;
   Without He stands, and asks to enter in:
   Why should He seek a shelter sad with sin?
Will He but knock and ask, and nothing more?

He knows what ways I take to shut my heart,
   And if He will He can Himself undo
   My foolish fastenings, or by force break through,
Nor wait till I fulfill my needless part.

But nay, He will not choose to enter so;
   He will not be my guest without consent,
   Nor, though I say, "Come in," is He content;
I must arise and ope, or He will go.

He shall not go; I do arise and ope—
   "Come in, dear Lord, come in and sup with me,

O blessèd Guest, and let me sup with Thee!"
Where is the door? for in this dark I grope,

And cannot find it soon enough; my hand,
   Shut hard, holds fast the one sure key I need,
   And trembles, shaken with its eager heed—
No other key will answer my demand.

The door between is some command undone;
   Obedience is the key that slides the bar,
   And lets Him in, who stands so near, so far;
The doors are many, but the key is one.

Which door, dear Lord? knock, speak, that I may know;
   Hark, heart! He answers with His hand and voice—
   Oh, still small sign, I tremble and rejoice,
Nor longer doubt which way my feet must go.

Full lief and soon this door would open too,
   If once my key would find the narrow slit,
   Which, being so narrow, is so hard to hit—
But lo! one little ray that glimmers through,

Not spreading light, but lighting to the light—
   Now steady, hand, for good speed's sake be slow,

One straight right aim, a pulse of pressure, so—
How small, how great, the change from dark to bright!

Now He is here, I seem no longer here;
   This place of light is not my chamber dim;
   It is not He with me, but I with Him,
And Host, not Guest, He breaks the bread of cheer.

I lie upon the bosom of my Lord,
   And feel His heart, and time my heart thereby;
   The tune so sweet, I have no need to try,
But rest and trust, and beat the perfect chord.

A little while I lie upon His heart,
   Feasting on love, and loving there to feast,
   And then, once more the shadows are increased
Around me, and I feel my Lord depart.

Again alone, but in a farther place,
   I sit with darkness, waiting for a sign;
   Again I hear the same sweet plea divine,
And suit outside of hospitable grace.

This is His guile—He makes me act the host
   To shelter Him, and lo! He shelters me;

Asking for alms, He summons me to be
A guest at banquets of the Holy Ghost.

So, on and on, through many an opening door
   That gladly opens to the key I bring,
     From brightening court to court of Christ
        my King,
Hope-led, love-fed, I journey evermore.

"FAR AWAY."

"The land that is very far off."—ISA. xxxiii. 17.

UPON the shore
   Of evermore
We sport like children at their play;
   And gather shells
   Where sinks and swells
The mighty sea from far away.

   Upon the beach
   Nor voice, nor speech
Doth things intelligible say;
   But through our souls
   A whisper rolls
That comes to us from far away.

   Into our ears
   The voice of years

"FAR AWAY."

Comes deeper, deeper, day by day,
    We stoop to hear,
    As it draws near,
Its awfulness from far away.

    At what it tells
    We drop the shells
We were so full of yesterday.
    And pick no more
    Upon that shore,
But dream of brighter far away.

    And o'er the tide,
    Far out and wide,
The yearnings of our souls doth stray;
    We long to go,
    We do not know
Where it may be, but far away.

    The mighty deep
    Doth slowly creep
Upon the shore where we did play;
    The very sand
    Where we did stand
A moment hence, swept far away.

    Our playmates all
    Beyond our call,
Are passing hence, as we too may,

Unto that shore
Of evermore,
Beyond the boundless far away.

We'll trust the wave,
And Him to save
Beneath whose feet as marble lay
The rolling deep,
For He can keep
Our souls in that dim far away.

"PURIFIETH HIMSELF EVEN AS HE IS PURE."

WHEN in deep silence my expectant heart,
Waited the sight of its adored guest
With lamp in hand, I urged a tireless quest
For soil, or stain; I sought to place my best
In every part.

The lamp-light fell athwart my closed rooms,
Like whitest linen gleamed the draperies.
Oh, fair shall shine each thing that in them is,
When on my night the Sun of Love shall rise
To light these glooms!

Soon with that day my windows were aglow:
I turned to look my ordered heart within,

Then drowned my pride in tears; for what had been
Pure in my eyes, was dyed with smut of sin—
    I kneeled low:

Lord, not myself, but Thou, must make me clean.
Let love, a river, flood these dusty floors;
Write Thy name on the lintels of the doors,
Then when again Thy searching sunshine pours,
    I *shall be* clean.

GOD KNOWETH BEST.

HE took them from me, one by one,
    The things I set my heart upon;
They looked so harmless, fair, and blest;
Would they have hurt me? God knows best;
He loves me so, He would not wrest
Them from me if it were not best.

He took them from me, one by one—
The friends I set my heart upon.
Oh! did they come, they and their love,
Between me and my Lord above?
Were they as idols in my breast?
It may be: God in heaven knows best.

I will not say, I did not weep,
As doth a child that wants to keep
The pleasant things in hurtful p ay
His wiser parent takes away:
But in this comfort I will rest,
He who hath taken knowe   best.

THE THORN AND CROSS.

"There was given unto me a thorn in the flesh."—2 Cor. xii. 7.

"And whosoever doth not bear his cross and come after me, cannot be my disciple."—St. Luke xiv. 27.

THE thorn is very sharp, O righteous Mas-
  ter!
  The flesh is weak;
And drops of blood and blinding tears fall
  faster
  Than I can speak!
Ah! deeply in my bosom it is driven
  To rend and tear,
Pressed by the rugged cross that Thou hast
  given
  For me to bear!

I could endure the thorn, though fiercely gall-
  ing,
  If that were all;
Or bear the cross without a fear of falling—

Yea, count it small
If I could only bear it on my shoulder,
And not my breast,
Where goads the thorn; my heart would then grow bolder,
Blest with such rest.

I had borne either, singly; both united
Have vanquished me!
I prostrate lie, oppressed, distressed, benighted,
And cry to Thee!
O Jesus! place Thy hand beneath the burden
A little while;
Or soothe the wounds by that all-healing guerdon,
A Saviour's smile!

He comes; He lifts; He soothes. A little longer
I plod my way!
His gracious strength has made my sad soul stronger
To last the day.
But cross and thorn will tempt, until the closing
Of mortal life;
And I shall show, although in heaven reposing,
The scars of strife.

GETHSEMANE.

LIKE Him, whilst friends and lovers slept,
  Have we not all heart-broken crept
Into thy shadows once and wept,
                    Gethsemane?

We knew not how the day had run,
We only knew that hope was gone,
And fain no more would greet the sun,
                    Gethsemane!

Our mothers slumbered in the tomb,
Love, though immortal, could not come
To cheer their children in thy gloom,
                    Gethsemane!

Not with us was our true helpmeet,
Who bore us sons and made life sweet,
And loved us with a love complete,
                    Gethsemane!

Not with us might the friend abide,
Who, ever trusty, ever tried,
Fought our Truth's battle by our side,
                    Gethsemane!

We were alone. The world was still,
The breath of heaven seemed cold and chill,
We beat our breast and wept our fill,
                    Gethsemane!

Prone on the ground our limbs were spread,
We wished it were our dying bed,
Since hope, and joy, and faith had fled,
> Gethsemane!

But late, there broke a little light
Into the darkness of the night,
And we were taught to pray aright,
> Gethsemane!

Then Christ Himself said, standing near,
" O fellow-mourners, have no fear,
I weep with thee, and God is here!"
> Gethsemane!

THEIR THOUGHTS AND OUR THOUGHTS.

SIX years have faded since she went away,
   Six years for her to live in heavenly places,
  To learn the look of blessèd angel faces;
Six years to grow as only angels may.

I wonder oft what she is doing there,
   By the still waters that forever flow;
   What mighty secrets she has come to know!
What graces won, divinely sweet and fair!

I wonder who of those that went before,
   And those that followed on her shining way,

She has met there, in Heaven's auroral day,
And if they talk their earth-life o'er and o'er?

I think this very morning they are met,
   She and one other only three years gone,
     In some dear place in Heaven, secure and lone,
To talk of things they never can forget.

For I am sure that naught of their new life,
   No grace or glory that is there revealed,
   The fountains of past love has ever sealed,
But these will ever be with sweetness rife.

I cannot think of them as they are now,
   Of the new light that shines upon their faces;
   I cannot image forth their angel graces;
And I am glad, so glad, that it is so.

So we will think of them just as they were,
   Their voices sweet and all their pleasant ways;
   And thoughts like these shall help us through the days,
Until we go to meet them where they are.

CONSOLATION IN CHRIST.

IF any consolation be
  In Christ! O, words of mild reproof
To all who sit in misery,
Holding their griefs and cares aloof
From that dear Helper,—bowing low
Beneath the heavy weights of woe;
Yet seeking not the sweet relief
To purchase which He bore our grief.

If there *no* consolation be
In Christ, or comfort in His love,
Ah! where for succor can we flee?
Too heavy must our burden prove
If we must bear its weight alone—
So deathly faint as we have grown;
Beneath this long suspense and fear,
What if there were no comfort near?

Alone, and all-forsaken by
The hearts that we have served in need,
While keen reproaches multiply,
And gaping wounds afresh do bleed,
If in the Spirit we can see
No fellowship of sympathy,
No tender pity of our need,
Then are we desolate indeed!

Comfort the hearts that ache and bleed,
O blessèd Jesus ! Soothe the woe
Of trembling lips that vainly plead ;
How rough these earthly paths can grow,
Thy piercèd, wounded feet attest ;
Give to the heavy-laden rest,
Draw all the weary unto Thee,
Till they Thy consolation see.

"HE LEADETH ME."

Psalm xxiii.

IN " pastures green ?" Not always ; sometimes He,
Who knoweth best, in kindness leadeth me
In weary ways, where heavy shadows be ;

Out of the sunshine warm and soft and bright,
Out of the sunshine into darkest night,
I oft would faint with sorrow and affright,

Only for this—I know He holds my hand ;
So, whether led in green or desert land,
I trust, although I may not understand.

And by " still waters ?" No, not always so ;
Ofttimes the heavy tempests round me blow,
And o'er my soul the waves and billows go.

But when the storms beat loudest, and I cry
Aloud for help, the Master standeth by,
And whispers to my soul, " Lo, it is I !"

Above the tempest wild I hear Him say,
" Beyond this darkness lies the perfect day ;
In every path of thine I lead the way."

So, whether on the hill-tops high and fair
I dwell, or in the sunless valleys where
The shadows lie—what matter? He is there.

And more than this : where'er the pathway lead,
He gives to me no helpless, broken reed,
But His own hand, sufficient for my need.

So, where He leads me, I can safely go ;
And in the blest hereafter I shall know,
Why in His wisdom He hath led me so.

REST.

"Oh ! spare me, that I may recover strength, before I go hence, and be no more."—Ps. xxxix. 13.

FOLD up thy hands, my weary soul,
    Sit down beside the way !
Thou hast at last a time to rest,
    At last a holiday.

Thy lingering life of weariness,
   Thy time of toil and tears,
A little space may grant thee grace
   To overcome thy fears.

A bright access of patient peace,
   Nor rapture, nor delight;
But even as sounds of labor cease
   Before the hush of night.

Or, as the storm that all day long
   Has wailed, and raged, and wept,
Nor ceased its force nor changed its course,
   While slow the daylight crept;

But suddenly, before the sun
   Drops down behind the hills,
A clear, calm shining parts the cloud,
   And all the ether fills.

Or, as the sweet and steadfast shore
   To them that sailed the sea;
Or home to them that ply the oar,
   Or leave captivity.

Like any child that cries itself
   On mother-breast to sleep,
Lord, let me lie a little while,
   Till slumber groweth deep;

So deep that neither love nor life
  Shall stir its calm repose—
Beyond the stress of mortal strife,
  The strain of mortal woes.

Spare me this hour to sleep, before
  Thy sleepless bliss is given;
Give me a day of rest on earth,
  Before the work of heaven!

I STAND AND KNOCK.

I STAND and knock, at holy Advent time;
    Oh! happy, then, is he
Who, knowing well the Shepherd's voice,
    Opens the door to me;
The evening meal with him I'll hold,
And heavenly light and grace unfold.
    I stand and knock.

I stand and knock. Without it is so cold;
    The snow lies o'er the land;
Like crystal columns, tall and straight,
    The icy fir-trees stand,
And frozen are the hearts of mortals.
Who will unloose the tight-barred portals?
    I stand and knock.

I stand and knock. Oh, could'st Thou look
      but once
    Into my very face!
Could'st Thou behold the crown of thorns,
    The bloody nail-prints trace!
  So long have I been seeking Thee,
  My steps lead from the accursed tree,
    I stand and knock.

I stand and knock. The evening is so calm,
    So quiet, near and far
The wide earth sleeps, from yonder heaven
    Looks down the evening star.
  In such still, sacred hour of night,
  To many a heart I've given light.
    I stand and knock.

I stand and knock. Say not, "It is the wind
    Rustling the branches sere;"
Thy Saviour 'tis, thy Lord, my child;
    Ah, close not now thine ear!
  Though now I speak in whispers mild,
  Too soon, perchance, in storm-blasts wild,
    I stand and knock.

I stand and knock. Now, would I be thy guest;
    But when this house of thine
A ruin lies, then think, oh! soul,
    That thou shalt knock at Mine.

Then, if thou hast welcomed *Me*,
I'll open Heaven's gates to *thee*.
   I stand and knock.

"*LET US PASS OVER.*"
Mark iv. 35.

"LET us pass over!" We were far astray;
 Between us and our home the sea was wide;
When He, who is Himself the blessèd way,
 Bade us cross over, and with Him abide.

Faith wavered, and temptation lured us on;
 Too fair, this world, for mortal to withstand;
Yet came His voice, though from Him we had gone:
 " Let us pass over to a better land."

Again our hearts were torn with grief and pain;
 Our eyes tear-blinded; life seemed only loss!
When, calling us to His pierced side again,
 Christ showed to us the *crown* beyond the *cross!*

And now life wanes. We stand by the dark river,
 With none beside save Him, the crucified.
Gently He calls, whose love is joy forever:
 " Let us pass over to the other side,"

PRAYING IN SPIRIT.

"But thou, when thou prayest, enter into thy closet."

I need not leave the jostling world,
    Or wait till daily tasks are o'er,
To fold my palms in secret prayer
    Within the close-shut closet door.

There is a viewless, cloistered room,
    As high as heaven, as fair as day,
Where, though my feet may join the throng,
    My soul can enter in and pray.

When I have banished wayward thoughts,
    Of sinful works the fruitful seed,
When folly wins my thoughts no more,
    The closet door is shut, indeed.

No human step approaching, breaks
    The blissful silence of the place;
No shadow steals across the light
    That falls from my Redeemer's face!

And never through those crystal walls
    The clash of life can pierce its way,
Nor ever can a human ear
    Drink in the spirit-words I say.

One hearkening, even, cannot know
   When I have crossed the threshold o'er,
For He alone who hears my prayer,
   Has heard the shutting of the door!

"SEALED."

I AM Thine own, O Christ—
   Henceforth entirely Thine!
And life, from this glad hour,
   New life is mine!

No earthly joy shall lure
   My quiet soul from Thee:
This deep delight, so pure,
   Is heaven to me.

My little song of praise
   In sweet content I sing;
To Thee the note I raise,
   My King! My King!

I cannot tell the art
   By which such bliss is given;
I know Thou hast my heart,
   And I—have heaven.

THE SPARROW'S TEXT.

A SPARROW lighted chirping on a spray
    Close to my window, as I knelt in prayer,
Bowed by a heavy load of anxious care.
The morn was bitter, but the bird was gay,
And seemed by cheery look and chirp to say,
    "What though the snow conceals my wonted fare,
Nor I have barn or store-house anywhere,
Yet I trust Heaven even on a winter's day?"
That little bird came like a winged text
    Flutt'ring from out God's Word to soothe my breast:
What though my life with wintry cares be vexed,
    On a kind Father's watchful love I rest;
He meets *this moment's need;* I leave the *next;*
And, always trusting, shall be always blest?

MY CROSS.

"O LORD, my God!" I oft have said,
    "Had I some other cross instead
Of this I bear from day to day,
'Twere easier to go on my way.

"I do not murmur at its weight;
    That Thou hast made proportionate

To my scant strength; but, oh! full sore
It presses where it pressed before.

"Change for a space, however brief,
The wonted burden, that relief
May o'er my aching shoulders steal,
And the deep bruise have room to heal!"

While thus I sadly sighed to-day,
I heard my gracious Father say,
"Canst thou not trust My love, my child,
And to thy cross be reconciled?

"I fashioned it thy needs to meet;
Nor were thy discipline complete
Without that very pain and bruise,
Which thy weak heart would fain refuse."

Ashamed, I answered, "As Thou wilt;
I own my faithlessness and guilt!
Welcome the weary pain shall be,
Since only that is best for me."

THE PILGRIM'S PRAYER.

I GO on pilgrimage. The road in view
    Lies fair revealed;
But, when the sun shall drink the wayside dew,
    Be Thou my Shield!

THE PILGRIM'S PRAYER.

The soft wind shifts, and lo! gray mists of doubt
    My pathway hide!
With bruisèd feet and hands I grope about;
    Be Thou my Guide!

Now tempests rise, and o'er the wind-swept way,
    To 'scape the shock,
Seeking some covert vainly as I stray,
    Be Thou my Rock!

Though after storm, stealing through sun-touched rift,
    Calm comes at length,
O'erborne and prone, mine eyes I may not lift;
    Be Thou my strength!

One draught from Thy life-giving fountain send,
    And let me quaff—
Refreshed, I'll gird me for my journey's end;
    Be Thou my Staff!

When pilgrimage is o'er, and life's day lies
    Low in the west—
While the night shadows dim my weary eyes,
    Be Thou my Rest!

I AND MY BURDEN.

I AND my burden, O Master!
   I come at Thy merciful call,
And cry to the Infinite goodness
   That helpeth and healeth us all.

I and my burden! I bore it
   In weakness and weariness long;
It dimmed all the glory of sunlight,
   It hushed all the sweetness of song.

It hid all the love-light around me,
   Dropped thorns on my wearisome way,
It benumbed all the strength of my striving,
   And banished the beauty of day.

I and my burden, O Master!
   No sheaves of the ripening grain;
But only a fruitage of folly,
   Of idleness, weakness, and pain.

I and my burden! I bring it
   In shame and in sorrow to Thee;
For I know there is none other refuge
   Of help, or of healing for me.

I stretch forth the hands that are failing,
   I lift up the heart that is sore;
I have brought Thee my burden, O Master!
   Thy pardon and peace I implore!

HEAVEN OVER ALL.

How many hours of patient toil
 Our faithfulness to test?
How many burdens yet to bear
 Before the hands may rest?
How many crosses ere they lie
 Calm folded on the breast?
Yet toil and burden, cross and rod,
 Divinest love hath blest.

How fierce the battle ere we win
 The conqueror's robe and palm!
How sharp the wounds before they feel
 The healing drops of balm!
How loud the Babel sounds of strife
 Before the evening psalm!
And yet, o'er all, the heaven extends
 Its soundless deeps of calm.

CUI BONO.

Pale star, if star thou be, that art
 So fain to shine, though far apart
  From all thy stately peers;
Thou whom the eye can scarce discern—
Oh! who hath set thee there to burn
  Among the spheres?

Thou com'st too late: the firmament
Is full, and thou wast never meant
    For yonder gorgeous steep;
The night hath counted all her pearls,
And pillow'd on her casket, furls
    Her wings in sleep.

The night needs not thy tardy ray;
Thou canst not usher in the day,
    Nor make the twilight fair;
What sailor turns to thee at sea?
What mourner doth look up to thee
    In his despair?

Mournful or glad, no eye shall chance
To light on thee; no curious glance
    Thy motions shall discern:
No lonely pilgrim pause to catch
Thy parting ray, nor lover watch
    For thy return.

Oh! leave the world that loves thee not—
For who shall mark the vacant spot?
    Oh! drop into the cloud
That waits to take thee out of sight,
Beyond the glare of yonder bright
    And chilly crowd.

"I may not, if I would, return
Into the dark, or cease to burn

My spark of life divine:
For He that in my lamp distills
The sacred oil, He surely wills
That I should shine.

" I fret not at the blaze of spheres,
The distant splendor that endears
The night to men ; but strive,
Finding strange bliss in perfect calm,
To keep with these few drops of balm
My flame alive.

" It may be that some vagrant world
Or aimless atom, toss'd and whirl'd
Through windy tracks of space,
Perceives by me the hand that tends
It ever, and the goal that ends
Its tedious race.

" I know not: me this only care
Concerns, that I forever bear
My silver lamp on high,
Nor lift to God a laggard flame,
Because on earth I cannot claim
A partial eye."

OLD AGE.

FLING down the faded blossoms of the spring,
   Nor clasp the roses with regretful hand;
The joy of summer is a vanished thing;
   Let it depart, and learn to understand
The gladness of great calm—the autumn rest,
The Peace—of human joys the latest and the best.

Ah! I remember how in early days
   The primrose and the wild-flower grew beside
My tangled forest paths, whose devious ways
   Filled me with joys of mysteries untried,
And terror that was more than half delight,
And sense of budding life, and longings infinite.

And I remember how, in Life's hot noon,
   Around my path the lavish roses shed
Color and fragrance, and the air of June
   Breathed rapture—now those summer days are fled;
Days of sweet peril, when the serpent lay
Lurking at every turn of life's enchanted way.

The light of spring, the summer's glow, are o'er,
   And I rejoice in knowing that for me

OLD AGE.

The woodbine and the roses bloom no more,
  The tender green is gone from field and
    tree;
Brown barren sprays stand clear against the
    blue,
And leaves fall fast, *and let the truthful sun-
    light through.*

For me the hooded herbs of autumn grow,
  Square-stemmed and sober; mint and sage,
Horehound and balm—such plants as healers
    know;
  And the decline of life's long pilgrimage
Is soft and sweet with marjoram and thyme.
Bright with pure evening dew, not serpents'
    glittering slime.

And round my path the aromatic air
  Breathes health and perfume, and the turfy
    ground
Is soft for weary feet, and smooth and fair
  With little thornless blossoms that abound
In safe dry places, where the mountain side
Lies to the setting sun, and no ill beast can
    hide.

What is there to regret? Why should I mourn
  To leave the forest and the marsh behind,
Or towards the rank, low meadows sadly turn?
  Since here another loveliness I find,

Safer and not less beautiful—and blest
   With glimpses, faint and far, of the long-
      wished-for Rest.

And so I drop the roses from my hand,
   And let the thorn-pricks heal, and take my
      way
Down hill, across a fair and peaceful land
   Lapt in the golden calm of dying day—
Glad that the night is near, and glad to know
That, rough or smooth the way, *I have not
      far to go.*

MY CROSS.

IT is not heavy, agonizing woe,
   Bearing me down with hopeless, crushing
      weight;
No ray of comfort in the gathering gloom;
   A heart bereaved, a household desolate.

It is not sickness with her withering hand,
   Keeping me low upon a couch of pain;
Longing each morning for the weary night,
   At night for weary day to come again.

It is not poverty with chilling blast,
   The sunken eye, the hunger-wasted form;
The dear ones perishing for lack of bread,
   With no safe shelter from the winter's storm.

MY CROSS.

It is not slander with her evil tongue;
  'Tis not "presumptuous sins" against my
    God;
Not reputation lost, nor friends betrayed;
  That such is not my cross I thank my God.

Mine is a daily cross of petty cares,
  Of little duties pressing on my heart,
Of little troubles hard to reconcile,
  Of inward troubles overcome in part.

My feet are weary in their daily rounds,
  My heart is weary of its daily care,
My sinful nature often doth rebel;
  I pray for grace my daily cross to bear.

It is not heavy, Lord, yet oft I pine;
  It is not heavy, but 'tis everywhere;
By day and night each hour my cross I bear,
  I dare not lay it down—Thou keep'st it there.

I dare not lay it down; I only ask
  That, taking up my daily cross, I may
Follow my Master, humbly, step by step,
  Through clouds and darkness, unto perfect
    day.

CLOSET PRAYER.

LORD, I have shut my door,
    Shut out life's busy cares and fretting noise:
Here in this silence they intrude no more;
    Speak Thou, and heavenly joys
Shall fill my heart with music sweet and calm,
    A holy psalm.

    Yes, I have shut my door
Even on all the beauty of Thine earth;
To its blue ceiling from its emerald floor,
    Filled with spring's bloom and mirth;
From these Thy works I turn, Thyself I seek,
    To Thee I speak.

    And I have shut my door
On earthly passions, all its yearning love,
Its tender friendships, all the priceless store
    Of human ties. Above
All these my heart aspires, O heart divine,
    Stoop Thou to mine!

    Lord, I have shut my door,
Come Thou and visit me. I am alone!
Come, as when doors were shut, Thou cam'st of yore
    And visitedst Thine own.
My Lord, I kneel with reverent love and fear,
    For Thou art here!

DAY.

"NOT clear, nor dark," not rain nor shine—
Lord, help a trembling child of Thine
    To sit, and sing, and wait:
Surely the days of light are Thine;
Thou hast not spent Thy store divine,
    Nor closed Thy golden gate.

But I would do, and I would go,
Would have, would see, would seek, would know,
    And Thou would'st have me wait;
Would'st have me rest, and trust, and smile,
And work at little things a while,
    Till Thou shalt give me great.

Content to be uncertain still,
To serve by waiting for Thy will,
    Through chilly, gloomy days—
To pray for doubting ones and tried,
Whose lives may have a darker side;
    To pray for grace to praise.

"Known to the Lord"—this dreary time
Shall do its part, and fruit of Thine,
    So precious, rare, and sweet,

Shall cluster on Thy trees of grace,
And make their home a sacred place
    For Thee and angels meet.

LEFT ALL.

MASTER, unto Thy feet my gifts I bring,
    Alas! how small;
I follow Thee, though far my wandering
    Ere I left all.

Thou knowest all the roughness of the road,
    The pain, the fear,
The desert sands my wayward feet have trod,
    The terrors near.

The evil hidden deep within my heart,
    The constant strife,
Ere I was drawn to choose the better part,
    The truer life.

If now Thine eye, that seeth all, can see
    A single love
That more than Thy sweet love is now to me,
    Oh! Friend above,

Help me to tear the idol from its place!
    For I would fain
Behold the beauty of my Saviour's face,
    And so remain

Through all the seasons of this changeful life,
  With lifted eye,
Unheeding though through sorrow and through
    strife—
  Thou comest nigh.

I have left all, and so I follow Thee;
  Oh! take my hand,
And by the way that seemest best for me,
  Lead to the land

Of light and love, where many mansions are:
  Streams not a ray,
Out through the vista of the gates ajar,
  O'er all my way!

WHY WALK IN DARKNESS?

WHY walk in darkness? Has the clear
    light vanished
  That gave us joy and day?
Has the great sun departed? Has sin ban-
    ished
  His life-begetting ray?

Light of the world! forever, ever shining,
  . There is no change in Thee;
True Light of life, all joy and health enshrin-
    ing,
  Thou canst not fade nor fl

Thou hast arisen; but Thou descendest never—
    To-day shines as the past;
All that Thou wast, Thou art, and shalt be ever—
    Brightness from first to last.

Night visits not Thy sky, nor storm, nor sadness;
    Day fills up all its blue:
Unfailing beauty, and unfaltering gladness,
    And love, forever new.

Why walk in darkness? Our true light still shineth;
    It is not night, but day.
All healing and all peace His light enshrineth;
    Why shun His loving ray?

Are night and shadows better, truer, dearer,
    Than day, and joy, and love?
Do tremblings and mistrusting bring us nearer
    To the great God of love!

Light of the world! undimming and unsetting,
    Oh, shine each mist away!
Banish the fear, the falsehood, and the fretting,
    By an unchanging day!

ADORATION.

I LOVE my God, but with no love of mine,
    For I have none to give;
I love Thee, Lord, but all the love is Thine,
    For by Thy life I live.
I am as nothing, and rejoice to be
Emptied, and lost, and swallowed up in Thee.

Thou, Lord, alone art all Thy children need,
    And there is none beside:
From Thee the streams of blessedness proceed,
    In Thee the blest abide,
Fountain of life, and all-abounding grace,
Our source, our centre, and our dwelling-place.

"GOD HATH HIS PLAN FOR EVERY MAN."

TAKE this maxim home to your heart,
    If groping in earth's shadows;
And the blossoms of faith and hope will start
    And brighten life's dreary meadows,
And the clouds give place to sunlight's gold,
    And the rocks grow green 'neath the mosses;
        "God hath His plan
           For every man."
Though mingled with flowers and crosses.

GOD'S PLAN.

Though weary and long the time may seem,
  Ere the veil of the future be lifted,
And many a radiant hope and dream
  Have into oblivion drifted;
Yet after a while the light will come,
  And after a while the glory;
     "God hath His plan
       For every man,"
  And the angels whisper the story.

Then why should ye murmur, and sigh, and fret,
  And follow each bent and calling?
The violet patiently waits to be wet
  With the dews at the night-time falling;
And the robin knows that the spring will come,
  Though the winds are around her wailing;
     "God hath His plan
       For every man,"
  And His ways are never-failing.

Then gird ye on the armor of faith,
  And onward your way keep pressing:
It may be through valleys of carnage and death,
  Or up on the Mount of Blessing;
And if by His counsel guided, at last
  He'll lead you up to your glory;
     "God hath His plan
       For every man,"
  And the angels whisper the story.

ENDURANCE.

FAINT not beneath thy burden, though it seem
Too heavy for thee, and thy strength be small;
Though the fierce raging of the noon-tide beam
On thy defenceless head untempered fall.

Though sad and heart-sick with the weight of woe,
That to the earth would crush thee—journey on;
What though it be with faltering step and slow,
Thou wilt forget the toil when rest is won.

Nay! murmur not, because no kindred heart
May share thy burden with thee—but alone
Still struggle bravely on, though all depart,
Is it not said that " Each must bear his own?"

All have not equally the power to bless;
And of the many few could cheer our lot;
For " the heart knoweth its own bitterness,
And with its joy a stranger meddleth not."

Then be not faithless though thy soul be dark;
Is not thy Master's seal upon thy brow?
Oft has His presence saved thy shining bark,
And thinkest thou He will forsake thee now?

Hath He not bid thee cast on Him thy care,
Saying He careth for thee? Then arise,
And on thy path, if trod in faith and prayer,
The thorns shall turn to flowers of Paradise.

"REMEMBER NOT THE SINS OF MY YOUTH."

COULD I recall the years that now are flown
      Forevermore;
Revive my early visions—long o'erthrown—
      And hope restore,
How blest it were to mould my life anew,
And all my broken vows of youth renew!

Oh! were I once again but free to choose
      As in past days,
How oft the sunlit path I would refuse
      For sterner ways!
Content to turn aside from every road
Save that which kept me in the smile of God.

But vain the dream: the strife is o'er with me;
      Dark days remain:
I could not trust my heart if I were free
      To choose again:
The dazzling morning might again deceive,
Life be misspent, and age be left to grieve.

I would not, if I could, recall the years
    That now are fled :
Their cares and pleasures, labors, hopes, and
    fears
    For me are dead :
I ask but mercy for the weary past,
And grace to guide me gently home at last.

JESUS ONLY.

"And when the voice was past, Jesus was found alone."—
    St. Luke ix. 36.

THE vision fades away—
    The brilliant radiance from heaven is
        gone ;
The angel visitants no longer stay,
    Silent the voice—Jesus is found alone.

In strange and sad amaze
    The three disciples watch, with longings vain,
While the cloud-chariot floats beyond their gaze ;
    Yes, these must go—He only will remain.

"Oh, linger, leave us not,
    Celestial Brothers! heaven has seemed so
        near
While ye were with us—earth was all forgot !"
    See, they have vanished ; He alone is here.

"He only—He, our own,
　Our loving Lord, is ever at our side,
What though the messengers of heaven are
　　　gone !
　Let all depart, if He may still abide !"

Such surely was their thought
　Who stood beside Him on that wondrous eve.
So would *we* feel ; Jesus, forsake us not,
　When those unutterably dear must leave !

For all their priceless love,
　All the deep joy their presence could impart,
Foretaste together of the bliss above,
　We thank Thee, Lord, though with a break-
　　　ing heart !

Nor murmur we to-day
　That He who gave should claim his own
　　　again ;
Long from their native heaven they could not
　　　stay,
　The servants go—the Master will remain.

Jesus is found alone—
　Enough for blessedness in earth or heaven !
Yet to our weakness hath His love made
　　　known,
　More than Himself shall in the end be given.

"Not lost, but gone before,"
Are our belovèd ones; the faithful Word
Tells of a meeting-place to part no more;
"So shall *we* be forever with the Lord!"

FAITH AND SIGHT IN THE LATTER DAYS.

THOU sayest, "Take up thy cross,
    O man, and follow me!"
The night is black, the feet are slack,
    Yet we would follow Thee.

But oh, dear Lord, we cry,
    That we Thy face could see!—
Thy blessèd face—one moment's space,
    Then might we follow Thee.

Dim tracts of time divide
    Those golden days from me;
Thy voice comes strange o'er years of change:
    How can we follow Thee?

Comes faint and far Thy voice,
    From vales of Galilee.
Thy vision fades in ancient shades:
    How should we follow Thee?

Unchanging law binds all,
    And nature all we see:
Thou art a star, far off, too far—
    Too far to follow Thee.

Ah, sense-bound heart and blind!
    Is naught but what we see?
Can time undo what once was true?
    Can we not follow Thee?

Is what we trace of law
    The whole of God's decree?
Does our brief span grasp Nature's plan,
    And bid not follow Thee?

O heavy cross of faith
    In what we cannot see!
As once of yore, Thyself restore,
    And help to follow Thee.

If not as once Thou cam'st
    In true humanity;
Come yet as guest within the breast
    That burns to follow Thee.

Within our heart of hearts
    In nearest nearness be;
Set up Thy throne within Thine own;
    Go, Lord—we follow Thee.

OUR HIGH PRIEST.
Heb. iv. 15.

TOUCHED with the feeling of our need!
My sad eyes weep for joy indeed;
For else, in all this round of pain,
How could they look on joy again?

Sad and cast down, O great High Priest,
Thou feelest what I feel the least;
And how much more this sore distress
That yearns so for Thy tenderness?

As once of old Thy gracious touch
Was laid for healing upon such;
So let me nearer press like them,
And reach and kiss Thy garment's hem.

I am so sick—oh, let me feel
One moment Thy sweet will to heal;
I am so tired—oh, let me rest,
Childlike, one hour upon Thy breast.

My heart is bruised with sorrow; see,
O Christ, how deep its wound may be!
Its want no other good can fill;
Its cry no other voice may still.

For Thou all human griefs hast known;
Hast trod earth's dreariest paths alone;
Hast loved and wept, by love denied,
And for Thy love been crucified.

Made perfect in Thine office so,
By each temptation, every woe,
Thou art Thyself of pain the balm,
And to the waves of sorrow, calm.

Touched with the feeling of my need,
O Saviour, be my Priest indeed!
Come near while life grows dim and chill,
And show Thyself the Healer still.

THE MOUNTAIN OF MYRRH.

Song of Solomon iv. 6.

UP to the fair myrrh mountain,
    The fresh frankincense hill,
I'll get me in this midnight,
    And drink of love my fill.
O hills of fragrance, smiling
    With every flower of love!
O slopes of sweetness, breathing
    Your odors from above!
Ye send me silent welcome,
    I waft you mine again;

Give me the wings of morning,
  Burst this still binding chain;
For soon shall break the day,
And shadows flee away.

There my beloved dwelleth,
  He calls me up to Him,
He bids me quit these valleys,
  These moorlands brown and dim.
There my long-parted wait me—
  The missed and mourned below;
Now, eager to rejoin them,
  I fain would rise and go.
Not long we here shall linger,
  Not long we here shall sigh;
The hour of dew and dawning
  Is hastening from on high;
For soon shall break the day,
And shadows flee away.

O streaks of happy day-spring,
  Salute us from above;
O never-setting sunlight,
  Earth longeth for thy love!
O hymns of unknown gladness,
  That hail us from the skies,
Swell till you gently silence
  Earth's meaner melodies!
O hope all hope surpassing,
  For evermore to be

O Christ, the Church's Bridegroom,
　In Paradise with Thee;
For soon shall break the day,
　And shadows flee away!

THE DIFFERENCE.

MEN send their ships, the eager things,
　To try their luck at sea,
But none can tell by note or count
　How many there may be.
One turneth east, another south—
　They never come again;
And then we know they must have sunk,
　But neither how nor when.

God sends His happy birds abroad—
　"They're less than ships," say we;
No moment passes but He knows
　How many there should be.
One buildeth high, another low,
　With just a bird's light care—
If only one, perchance, doth fall,
　God knoweth when and where.

HOW LONG?

My God, it is not fretfulness
   That makes me say, " How long?"
It is not heaviness of heart
   That hinders me in song;
'Tis not despair of truth and right,
   Nor coward dread of wrong.

But how can I, with such a hope
   Of glory and of home,
With such a joy before my eyes,
   Not wish the time were come—
Of years the jubilee, of days
   The Sabbath and the sun?

These years, what ages have they been!
   This life, how long it seems!
And how can I, in evil days,
   'Mid unknown hills and streams,
But sigh for those of home and heart,
   And visit them in dreams?

Yet peace, my heart, and hush, my tongue;
   Be calm, my troubled breast,
Each hurrying hour is hastening on,
   The everlasting rest;
Thou knowest that the time thy God
   Appoints for thee is best.

Let faith, nor fear, nor fretfulness,
  Awake the cry, " How long ? "
Let no faint-heartedness of soul
  Damp thy aspiring song ;
Right comes, truth dawns, and night departs
  Of error and of wrong.

" BOWING TO GOD'S WILL."

WHATE'ER God wills, let that be done,
  His will is ever wisest ;
His grace will all thy hope outrun,
  Who to that faith arisest.
    The gracious Lord
    Will help afford ;
He chastens with forbearing ;
    Who God believes,
    And to Him cleaves,
Shall not be left despairing.

My God is my sure confidence,
  My light and my existence ;
His counsel is beyond my sense,
  But stirs no weak resistance ;
    His Word declares
    The very hairs

Upon my head are numbered;
    His mercy large
    Holds me in charge
With care that never slumbered.

There comes a day, when, at His will,
    The pulse of nature ceases;
I think upon it and am still,
    Let come whate'er He pleases.
    To Him I trust
    My soul, my dust,
When flesh and spirit sever;
    The Christ we sing
    Has plucked the sting
Away from death forever.

THE SHADOW OF DEATH.

Suggested by Holman Hunt's Picture.*

WEARY, half weary of the work of life,
    The just begun and never ended strife,
      O Son of Mary!

---

* In this picture, Christ is represented as a young man working in a carpenter's shop at the close of the day. Weary with labor, He stretches His arms above His head. The action throws upon the wall behind His shadow, resembling that of one hanging upon a cross. His mother, kneeling before a casket, where she has been examining the crowns brought by the Wise Men of the East, starts to see the omen.

Jesus of Nazareth, the carpenter,
God-given, twenty years agone, to her,
      His mother Mary.
Jesus, the Lord's Anointed, free from sin;
The Way, by which a far-off heaven we win,
The Door, through which we may all enter in,
      Christ, Son of Mary!

Our days, Thou knowest, are short and full of woes,
Our cross, like Thine, too soon its shadow throws,
      Tired Son of Mary!
Our birth-crowns, that our mothers treasure up,
Are melted oft into one bitter cup—
      They drink, like Mary!
And with dim, frightened eyes, they also see
The shadow of some strange, accursed Tree,
Where their dear sons give up the ghost, like Thee,
      Great Son of Mary!

Oh, full of life, with all life's lawful joys
Calling upon Thee in melifluous noise,
      Fair Son of Mary!
Full of man's strength to do God's whole behest,
The noon-tide labor bringing evening rest,
      Sweet Son of Mary!

Yet through all this, love wiser far than these,
The shadow of the Cross Thy mother sees
In its unfathomable mysteries—
      Heart-piercèd Mary!

But Thou, with those Divine eyes, free from
    fear,
Thou seest the rest, remaining even here
      To Thee—and Mary!
And all God's people, all His children poor,
Whom thou namest brethren; knocking at
    their door,
      Blessèd Son of Mary!
And by and by, Thy earthly travail done,
Death consummating what Thy life begun,
Thou'lt say, "Come unto Me, each weary one—
      I am Son of Mary!"

O Son of God! and yet the woman's seed,
Bruise Thou our serpent sins, even though we
    bleed,
      Like Thee and Mary!
Forgive, if we, too, tired ere work be done,
Look forward longing to the set of sun,
      Alone—no, Mary!
And in the day of evil, anguish-rife,
Remember us! Through this, our mortal strife,
Lead us unto Thine everlasting life,
      Christ, Son of Mary!

ANYWHERE.

ANY little corner, Lord,
   In Thy vineyard wide,
Where Thou bidd'st me work for Thee,
   There I would abide;
Miracle of saving grace
That Thou givest me a place
     Anywhere.

Where we pitch our nightly tent
   Surely matters not;
If the day for Thee is spent,
   Blessèd is the spot;
Quickly we the tent may fold,
Cheerful march through storm and cold,
     With Thy care.

All along the wilderness,
   Let us keep our sight
On the moving pillar fixed,
   Constant day and night;
Then the heart will make its home,
Willing, led by Thee, to roam
     Anywhere.

THE SUFFERER'S COUCH.

To live, and not to die!
   Only to wait and wait;
To watch the passing of other feet
   Within the heavenly gate,
   To see the kindling light
   On many a long-loved face,
As one after one the Master calls
   Up to the higher place.

   To feel the loosened clasp;
   To catch the parting smile—
To hear the whisper from dying lips,
   "Only a little while!"
   Only—and yet we weep,
   God hides them from our love.
It sometimes seems too hard to rejoice
   That they are there—above.

   To live, and not to die!
   To suffer, not to reign,
Out in the dreary dark with the night,
   To wrestle hard with pain.
   They with the crown of peace
   Fair on each calmèd brow,
We with the sharpness of thorn and cross,
   To fight on still below.

Silence! O restless heart,
   In quietness be strong!
Well knoweth the Lord who watcheth thee,
   The pain of suffering long.
   He knoweth—yet His love
   Is stronger than thy tears;
Shall He let thee miss thy full reward,
   For all thy coward fears?

   Many a boat would sail
     Into the shining west;
Into the haven where she would be—
   The land of quiet rest.
   But o'er the darkening sea,
   Through mist, and cold, and fear,
Cometh sweet a voice that biddeth peace:
   "Patience—thy Lord is here."

WAITING FOR THE KING.

WE sit alone in the stillness,
   My soul and I,
And hear, outside of our cloister,
   The world go by—
The world, with its toiling and buying,
   And striving for gain;
The pitiful world, with its crying
   And moaning for pain.

We have no part in its aching,
    My soul and I ;
No part in its giving and taking,
    So let it go by.
We have shaken off from our sandals
    The dust of its mart,
And smile to think of its tumult,
    Where we sit apart.

Closed are the portals forever,
    Lest any come in
To soil the snow of our vesture
    With fingers of sin ;
But lost in visions supernal
    We wait till the King
The gates of the city eternal
    Wide open shall swing.

"HE KNOWETH YE HAVE NEED."

ACROSS the discord of our lives comes lowly
One harmony our hearts too seldom heed,
The comfort given us by the Teacher holy :
    "He knoweth ye have need."

He sends the dew-drop for the flowers' drinking ;
He slants His sunshine on the waiting grain ;

And when the leaves with summer's heat are
    shrinking
  He giveth them His rain.

Good gifts from out His ever-open hand
  On everything around are freely thrown;
And thinkest thou, O heart, He will withstand
  Thy prayer alone?

O men and women, saddened in the living,
  Smiles on the lip and sorrow in the heart,
Open your souls more fully for receiving:
  Accept your part.

Sad, aching eyes, that through the mists of
    sorrow
  See all things by your blindness rendered
    dim,
Grief lasts to-day, but joy shall come to-morrow;
  Look up! and trust in Him.

For still that sweet voice of the Father's sending,
  Of Him who knows how human hearts can
    bleed,
Says to the weary ones before Him bending,
  " He knoweth ye have need;"

Knoweth the need and careth for the needing,
　Although His way is seldom quite our way,
And smiles to see how sadly we are treading
　The path that leads to-day.

Then unto our greatest need replying,
　That need of rest which every soul doth keep,
Upon His breast, like little children lying,
　He giveth us His sleep.

PENITENTIAL HYMN.

AS Mary knelt, and dropped her tears,
　So, gracious Lord, would we;
And pour the ointment of our hearts,
　Our choicest love, on Thee.

Oh, the sweet joys of penitence!
　We trust Thee, and adore;
We wonder at Thy gracious word,
　"Arise, and sin no more."

Thou dost forget our sinful past,
　Thou takest off the stain;
Bathed in the ocean of Thy love,
　Our souls are pure again.

We come with sad, confessing lips,
　For Thy forgiving touch;

And Thou dost thrill us with the words,
  That we have loved Thee much.

We raise our tearful eyes to Thee,
  And meet Thy smile divine;
Where shall we look, O pitying Christ!
  For tenderness like Thine?

We hide our souls in Thee, O Lord!
  In Thee we seek our rest;
Oh! raise us from Thy sacred feet,
  To lean upon Thy breast.

PREVENTING MERCIES.

Psalm lxxix. 8.

THE hawthorn hedge that keeps us from intruding,
  Looks very fierce and bare
When stripped by winter, every branch protruding
  Its thorns that wound and tear.

But spring-time comes; and like the rod that budded,
  Each twig breaks out in green;
And cushions soft of tender leaves are studded,
  Where spines alone are seen.

And honeysuckle, its bright wreath upbearing,
   The prickly top adorns;
Its golden trumpets victory declaring
   Of blossoms over thorns.

Nature in this mute parable unfoldeth
   A lesson sweet to me;
God's goodness in reproof my eye beholdeth,
   And His severity.

There is no grievous chastening but combineth
   Some brightness with the gloom;
Round every thorn in the flesh there twineth
   Some wreath of softening bloom.

The sorrows that to us seem so perplexing,
   Are mercies kindly sent,
To guard our wayward souls from sadder vex-
      ing,
   And greater ills prevent.

Like angels stern, they meet us when we wander
   Out of the narrow track,
With sword in hand, and yet with voices tender,
   To warn us quickly back.

We fain would eat the fruit that is forbidden,
   Not heeding what God saith;
But by these flaming cherubim we're chidden,
   Lest we should pluck our death.

To save us from the pit, no screen of roses
    Would serve for our defense,
The hindrance that completely interposes
    Stings back like thorny fence.

At first, when smarting from the shock, complaining
    Of wounds that freely bleed,
God's hedges of severity us paining,
    May seem severe indeed.

No tender veil of heavenly verdure brightens
    The branches fierce and bare;
No sun of comfort the dark sky enlightens,
    Or warms the wintry air.

But *afterwards*, God's blessed spring-time cometh,
    And bitter murmurs cease;
The sharp severity that pierced us bloometh,
    And yields the fruits of peace.

The Wreath of Life its healing leaves discovers
    Twined round each wounding stem,
And climbing by the thorns, above them hovers
    Its flowery diadem.

The last Great Day, each secret deep revealing,
    Shall teach us what we owe

To these *preventing mercies*, thus concealing
 Themselves in masks of woe;

What sunken rocks they showed, on which unwitting
 Our souls would have been wrecked;
What deadly sins they kept us from committing,
 What lust and pride they checked.

Then let us sing, our guarded way thus wending,
 Life's hidden snares among,
Of mercy and of judgment sweetly blending;
 Earth's sad but lovely song.

REST.

"Thou hast made us for Thyself, and the heart never resteth till it findeth rest in Thee."—St. Augustine.

MADE for Thyself, O God!
 Made for Thy love, Thy service, Thy delight;
Made to show forth Thy wisdom, grace, and might;
Made for Thy praise, whom veiled archangels laud!
O strange and glorious thought, that we may be
 A joy to Thee!

  Yet the heart turns away
From the grand destiny of bliss, and deems
'Twas made for its poor self, for passing dreams.
Chasing illusions, melting day by day,
Till, *for ourselves*, we read on this world's best:
  "This is not rest!"

  Nor can the vain toil cease,
Till, in the shadowy maze of life, we meet
One who can guide our aching, wayward feet
To find Himself—our Way, our Life, our Peace.
In Him, the long unrest is soothed and stilled;
  Our hearts are filled.

  O rest so true, so sweet!
Would it were shared by all the weary world!
'Neath shadowing banner of His love unfurled
We bend to kiss the Master's piercèd feet,
Then lean our love upon His boundless breast,
  And know God's rest!

COMMUNION HYMN.

"This man receiveth sinners, and eateth with them."—
LUKE xv. 2.

NOT worthy, Lord, to gather up the crumbs
  With trembling hand that from Thy
  table fall,

COMMUNION HYMN.

A weary heavy-laden sinner comes
   To plead Thy promise and obey Thy call.

I am not worthy to be thought Thy child,
   Nor sit the last and lowest at Thy board;
Too long a wanderer, and too oft beguiled,
   I only ask one reconciling word.

One word from Thee, my Lord, one smile, one
     look,
   And I could face the cold, rough world again;
And with that treasure in my heart could brook
   The wrath of devils and the scorn of men.

And is not mercy Thy prerogative;
   Free mercy, boundless, fathomless, Divine?
Me, Lord, the chief of sinners, me forgive!
   And Thine the greater glory, only Thine.

I hear Thy voice; Thou bidst me come and
     rest.
   I come, I kneel, I clasp Thy piercèd feet;
Thou bidst me take my place, a welcome guest
   Among Thy saints, and of Thy banquet eat.

My praise can only breathe itself in prayer,
   My prayer can only lose itself in Thee;
Dwell Thou forever in my heart, and there,
   Lord, let me sup with Thee; sup Thou with me.

THE PERFECT DAY.

"Until the day break and the shadows flee away."—CANTICLES xi. 17.

DARK is the sky that overhangs my soul,
The mists are thick that through the valley roll,
But as I tread I cheer my heart and say,
When the day breaks the shadows flee away.

Unholy phantoms from the deep arise,
And gather through the gloom before mine eyes;
But all shall vanish at the dawning ray;
When the day breaks the shadows flee away.

I bear the lamp my Master gave to me,
Burning and shining must it ever be,
And I must tend it till the night decay,
Till the day break and shadows flee away.

He maketh all things good unto His own,
For them in every darkness light is sown:
He will make good the gloom of this my day,
Till that day break and shadows flee away.

I GAZED UPON THE BITTER CROSS.

I GAZED upon the bitter Cross, and sought
  My spirit to subdue to mournfulness,
  That I might follow in His deep distress
The wounded Lamb of God; but vainly brought,
My will to sadness—every grieving thought
  Turned to a holy calm of thankfulness.

I thought on Pain, and straightway answered
    Peace,
  On Death, but Life immortal made reply.
  The tears of sorrow gathered in mine eye.
Only to feel sweet Comfort bid them cease;
Evermore Faith would thoughts of Love increase,
  Through every cloud still gleamed cerulean sky.

I sought, O Jesus, to be sad with Thee,
  And thus I learned the secret of Thy woe;
  That it was mine, Thou camest down to know
That I the fullness of Thy joy might see;
That Thy sore trial might bring rest to me;
  Waters of comfort from the pierced Rock flow.

I took the Cross which came to me, to bear,
   Praying for patience 'neath its heaviness,
   For strength to struggle on in weariness;
For my Lord's sake His rugged path to share;
And lo! upon the twilight of my ease,
   Broke the calm morning light of blessedness.

Thus, if we would His consolations prove,
   In taking up our Cross, we lay it down,
   For He doth haste to make it all His own;
Our enmity doth reconcile with love;
Affliction ever softening from above,
   And holding in our sight a heavenly crown.

FAITH.

I THANK Thee, Lord, that Thou hast kept
    The best in store;
We have enough, yet not too much
    To long for more;
A yearning for a deeper peace
    Not known before.

I thank Thee, Lord, that here our souls,
    Though amply blest,
Can never find, although they seek,
    A perfect rest—
Nor ever shall, until they lean
    On Jesus' breast.

HEART VENTURES.

I STOOD and watched my ships go out
   Each one by one, unmooring free,
What time the quiet harbor filled
   With flood-tide from the sea.

The first that sailed, her name was Joy,
   She spread a smooth, white, ample sail;
And eastward drove with bending spars
   Before the singing gale.

Another sailed, her name was Hope,
   No cargo in her hold she bore;
Thinking to find in Western lands
   Of merchandise a store.

The next that sailed, her name was Love,
   She showed a red flag at the mast—
A flag as red as blood she showed,
   And she sped South right fast.

The last that sailed, her name was Faith,
   Slowly she took her passage forth;
Tacked and lay-to: at last she steered
   A straight course for the North,

My gallant ships they sailed away,
   O'er the shimmering summer sea,

I stood at watch for many a day—
    But one came back to me.

For Joy was caught by Pirate Pain—
    Hope ran upon a hidden reef—
And Love took fire and foundered fast
    In whelming seas of Grief.

Faith came at last, storm-beat and torn,
    She recompensed me all my loss;
For as a cargo safe she brought
    A crown linked to a cross.

THE SILENT GOD.

O'ER all the world the church spire rocks,
    As swing the bells and strike the clocks
    To peal the passing of the year!
On God's great clock-tower in the skies,
Profoundest midnight silence lies;
No clangor from its bells arise;
    No faintest sound we hear.

Our coarse contrivances alike
Mark time with noisy tick and strife,
    Loud peal or solemn toll.
But noiseless on its axis turns
The earth. The sun how silent burns

Through heaven! A silent God, who learns
    His lessons to the soul.

No cry rings, therefore, from His lips,
When time is marked by sun's eclipse
    On Heaven's illumined dial-plate!
No sounds the seasons make as they
Succeed each other. None as day
Falls full on earth. Nor soars its spray
    When night's dark deluge doth abate.

O still, small voice! Thy whisper wakes
More surely than though thunder breaks
    To tell the year has fled!
By Thee, from death aroused, I cry,
Give now my after life, that I
May serve Thee now as when, on high,
Unmarked the years shall live and die,
    And time, with death, be dead!

GROW NOT OLD.

NEVER, my heart, wilt thou grow old!
    My hair is white, my blood runs cold,
And one by one my powers depart,
But youth sits smiling in my heart.

Downhill the path of age? O no,
Up, up, with patient steps I go;

I watch the skies fast brightening there,
I breathe a sweeter, purer air.

Beside my road small tasks spring up,
Though but to hand the cooling cup,
Speak the true word of hearty cheer,
Tell the lone soul that God is near.

Beat on, my heart, and grow not old!
And when thy pulses all are told,
Let me, though working, loving still,
Kneel as I meet my Father's will.

EVERY DAY.

O TRIFLING task so often done,
    Yet ever to be done anew!
O cares which come with every sun,
    Morn after morn, the long years through!
      We sink beneath their paltry sway—
      The irksome calls of every day.

The restless sense of wasted power,
    The tiresome sound of little things,
Are hard to bear, as hour by hour
    Its tedious iteration brings;
      Who shall evade or who delay
      The small demands of every day?

EVERY DAY.

The boulder in the torrent's course
  By tide and tempest lashed in vain,
Obeys the wave-whirled pebble's force,
  And yields its substance grain by grain;
    So crumble strongest lives away
    Beneath the wear of every day.

Who finds the lion in his lair,
  Who tracks the tiger for his life,
May wound them ere they are aware,
  Or conquer them in desperate strife,
    Yet powerless he to scathe or slay
    The vexing gnats of every day.

The steady strain that never stops
  Is mightier than the fiercest shock;
The constant fall of water-drops
  Will groove the adamantine rock;
    We feel our noblest powers decay,
    In feeble wars with every day.

We rise to meet a heavy blow—
  Our souls a sudden bravery fills—
But we endure not always so
  The drop by drop of little ills;
    We still deplore and still obey
    The hard behests of every day.

The heart which boldly faces death
  Upon the battle-field, and dares

Cannon and bayonet, faints beneath
  The needle-points of frets and cares;
    The stoutest spirits they dismay
    The tiny stings of every day.

And even saints of holy fame,
  Whose souls by faith have overcome,
Who wore amid the cruel flame
  The molten crown of martyrdom,
    Bore not without complaint alway
    The petty pains of every day.

Ah, more than martyr's aureole,
  And more than hero's heart of fire,
We need the humble strength of soul
  Which daily toils and ills require;—
    Sweet Patience! grant us, if you may,
    An added grace for every day!

LORD, HELP ME!

THE way seems dark about me; overhead
  The clouds have long since met in gloomy
    spread;
And when I looked to see the day break through,
Cloud after cloud came up with volume new.

And in that shadow I have passed along,
Feeling myself grow weak as it grew strong;

LORD, HELP ME!

Walking in doubt, and searching for the way,
And often at a stand—as now to-day.

And if before me on the path there lies
A spot of brightness from imagined skies,
Imagined shadows fall across it too,
And the far future takes the present's hue.

Perplexities do throng upon my sight,
Like scudding fog-banks, to obscure the light;
Some new dilemma rises every day,
And I can only shut my eyes and pray.

Lord, I am not sufficient for these things,
Give me the light that Thy sweet presence brings!
Give me Thy grace, give me Thy constant strength:
Lord, for my comfort now appear at length!

It may be that my way doth seem confused,
  Because *my* heart of *Thy* way is afraid;
Because my eyes have constantly refused
  To see the only opening Thou hast made.

Because my will would cross some flowery plain,
  When Thou hast thrown a hedge from side to side;
And turneth from the stormy walk of pain,
  Its trouble or its ease not even tried.

If thus I try to force my way along,
   The smoothest road encumbered is for me,
For were I as an angel, swift and strong,
   I could not go unless allured by Thee.

And now, I pray Thee, Lord, to lead Thy child—
   Poor wretched wanderer from Thy grace and love—
Whatever way Thou pleasest through the wild,
   So it but take her to Thy home above.

CLEANSING FIRES.

LET thy gold be cast in the furnace;
   Thy red gold precious and bright;
Do not fear the hungry fire,
   With its caverns of burning light:
And thy gold shall return more precious,
   Free from every spot and stain;
For gold must be tried by fire,
   And a heart must be tried by pain!

In the cruel fire of sorrow
   Cast thy heart, do not faint or wail:
Let thy hand be firm and steady,
   Do not let thy spirit quail;
But wait till the trial is over,
   And take thy heart again;
For as gold is tried by fire,
   So a heart must be tried by pain!

I shall know by the gleam and glitter
    Of the golden chain you wear,
By your heart's calm strength in loving,
    Of the fire they have had to bear.
Beat on, true heart, for ever
    Shine bright, strong golden chain;
And bless the cleansing fire,
    And furnace of living pain!

TWILIGHT.

BEND down from heaven, Almighty Love;
    The fullness of Thy grace impart;
Fold Thy soft wings, Eternal Dove,
    Over my weary heart!

The day is ended; all its pain
    And all its sin are known to Thee;
Heal Thou the wound, make white the stain,
    My burdened soul set free.

Enough of sorrow and of sin;
    I put the weary thoughts away:
The door is open now; come in,
    O Heavenly Guest, and stay!

Be Thou my teacher; let me learn;
    Here at Thy feet my place shall be;

Like Mary, I would gladly turn
    From earthly cares to Thee.

The sunset sky is bright and clear;
    A crimson sea with shores of gold;
So soft the hues, we need not fear
    Their glory to behold.

The blinding splendor of the sun
    Is here revealed to mortal sight;
So Thou, O Father, art made known
    In Christ, the Light of Light!

Thy power in Nature I can trace,
    Thy justice in my trembling heart;
But only in the Saviour's face
    I see Thee as Thou art.

O Son of God! O Truth divine!
    With warming grace my soul restore;
Lighten my darkness, rise and shine,
    Both now and evermore.

ASPIRATIONS.

AH, Lord! to be
    The least of all that wait on Thee;
To stand as one

ASPIRATIONS.

Whose loins are girt with power to run
  The appointed race,
Upheld by meekness, truth, and grace;
  To whom, beside,
All else with Christ is crucified,
  And loss is gain;
To whom Thy love is Peace in pain,
  As one who hears—
Beyond the tumult of the years,
  The strife, the sin,
The tribulation, toil, and tears,—
  Thy words of mercy, "Enter in!"

  Ah, Lord! that I may be
This chosen vessel meet for Thee;
  That I, so poor,
May joy o'er Thy great wealth in store;
  That I, so frail, weak,—utterly—
May strengthened be of Thine and Thee;
  That I, so vile,
May yet rejoice me in the smile
Of Him who died the death for me;—
  That I, indeed, may feel
The Lord my passionate appeal will hear;
And in His own good time make clear
Of these my torments, Doubt and Fear.

  But what am I

To stand without and call and cry?
   Behold, I plead,
In this mine hour of utmost need,
The unimaginable pain
Of Him, the guiltless, scourged, and slain
   For me.
O Lamb of God, mine eyes to Thee
   I lift, as one
Who watcheth for the morning sun—
   In mercy visit me!

   I stand awhile
To view, beneath the dim defile,
Through which the Lord my doubtful way
Hath wrought from darkness into day:
And shall I falter here?
   I stand before
   The temple door,
And wait until my Lord appear.

   For this I surely know:
The grace of Jesus hitherto,
   Alone, hath kept
Me in the dark where conscience slept:
   And straight and plain
Through all the past, or peace or pain,
   I mark and prove
The guiding of the Lord of Love.

Lord Jesus grant me grace
And meekness in Thy Holy Place;
A spirit fine
To cleave the gross, and calm resign
My very life, if life it be,
That separates my soul and Thee.

WAITING FOR JESUS.

"Jesus, I wait!" Last words breathed soft and low
From dying lips grown tremulous and faint:
O great Life-giver, Thou didst surely know
The yearnings of Thy Saint!

Waiting—a moment only—just a pause,
A hush before the music had begun;
A silence ere the cloudy veil withdraws,
And the bright Home is won.

"Jesus, I wait!" Was He not waiting, too,
With hands outstretched in welcome, and with eyes
Brimful of love, to guide His servant through
The gates of Paradise?

O calm, safe rest; all sorrows passed away
Like twilight mists before a risen moon;

O blessèd close to life's most weary day,
   O peace, attained so soon!

Teach us to live, and, living, wait for Thee,
   Redeemer—making life and labor sweet;
Watching and working till our eyes shall see
   Thy face they long to greet.

Our highest earthly bliss to do Thy will;
   Our hope, the promise of Thy great reward;
Our effort, all Thy purpose to fulfill,
   And magnify the Lord.

Teach us to wait,—as waits the ripened corn
   In golden fullness for the reaper's hand;
Wait for Thy garner, when the harvest morn
   Dawns o'er the weary land.

And Thou wilt come with radiant angel train,
   Lord of the harvest, claiming all Thine own.
Then shall we greet our dearest ones again,
   And know as we are known.

Then shall the endless Festival begin,
   And the long waiting as a dream go past;
For love, triumphant over death and sin,
   Shall reign supreme at last.

AN EVENING PRAYER.

MY Father! God of life and light,
   Ere evening's hour hath ebb'd away,
Before Thy throne of grace to-night
   I offer up this closing day.

Fresh from Thy hand, this morn it rose
   Divinely fair, sublimely meet;
I bring it back at evening's close,
   Alas! how changed, how incomplete!

One plea alone my heart can claim
   For such a tribute, soil'd and dim;
I offer it in Jesu's name,
   Make Thou its darkness light in Him.

I bring Thee all this day hath brought,
   Its storms and sunshine, joy and pain;
Its every word and deed and thought;
   Its hope and fear, its loss and gain.

I bring to Thee, to purify,
   Its few faint thoughts of Thee and Heaven;
I bring Thee all its tears to dry,
   And all its sins to be forgiven.

I lay before Thy pitying gaze

Its joys to bless, its wounds to cure;
I bring it all to speak Thy praise,
   And tell of Thy compassion sure.

And now, O Lord my God, or ere
   This day in sleep forgotten be,
Its dying breath must rise in prayer,
   And bear my latest thought to Thee!

And since, perchance, no morrow's light
   May greet mine ear with wakening call,
In Thy good care I leave this night
   Myself, my life, my heart, mine all!

The loved ones, those I hold so dear,
   Be pleased, sweet Lord, to guard and keep!
To all their hearts this night draw near,
   And tend and bless them while they sleep.

My human love, so incomplete,
   Where can its longings find their rest,
Except to lay them at Thy feet,
   Who knowest all, and lovest best?

On eyes that weep, on hearts that bleed,
   May all Thy richest blessings fall;
I ask Thy help for all who need,
   And asking this, I pray for all.

And if to morn in safety brought,
  Grant that sweet breathings, pure and true,
May rest on each awakening thought,
  As on fresh flowers the early dew.

Thus, Lord, this night I yield to Thee ;
  Or if I sleep, or if I wake,
Whate'er I have, whate'er I be,
  Bid me good-night for Jesus' sake.

SCHOOL LIFE.

I SAT in the school of sorrow,
  The Master was teaching there ;
But my eyes were dim with weeping,
  And my heart was full of care.

Instead of looking upward
  And seeing His face divine,
So full of the tenderest pity
  For weary hearts like mine,

I only thought of the burdens,
  The cross that before me lay,
So hard and heavy to carry
  That it darkened the light of day.

So, I could not learn my lesson,

And say, *Thy will be done;*
And the Master came not near me
As the weary hours went on.

At last, in my weary sorrow,
  I looked from the cross above;
And I saw the Master watching
  With a glance of tender love.

He turned to the cross before me,
  And I thought I heard Him say:
"My child, thou must bear thy burden,
  And learn thy task to-day.

"I may not tell the reason,
  'Tis enough for thee to know
That I, the Master, am teaching,
  And give this cup of woe."

So I stooped to that weary sorrow;
  One look at that face Divine
Had given me power to trust Him,
  And say, *Thy will, not mine.*"

And thus I learned my lesson,
  Taught by the Master alone;
He only knows the tears I shed,
  But He has wept His own.

And from them come a brightness
   Straight from the Home above,
Where the School Life will be ended,
   And the cross will show the love.

THE FAINTING HEART.

O HEART that, sad and weary,
   Dost count thy load too great,
Thy night too dark and dreary,
   The way too desolate;
Take comfort in Thy sorrow,
   God sets an end to woe;
There comes a happy morrow,
   A day thy Lord doth know.

Not clear nor dark that morning,
   That time not day nor night;
Peace broods upon its dawning,
   Secure and infinite.
It sees no clouds o'ercasting
   Its sunshine evermore;
No tears, no pain, no fasting,
   The vigil eve is o'er.

For shame thou shalt have double,
   For one deep sob of woe,
One moment sore of trouble,

Eternal bliss shall know.
There endless is thy pleasure,
　There countless is thy gain,
Past all degree and measure,
　Reward shall comfort pain.

No more with grief and sighing
　Thou drawest painful breath;
There shall be no more crying,
　There shall be no more death.
Such festival is holden
　Where all God's saints shall be,
Where seers and prophets olden
　Shall keep the feast with thee.

ART THOU WEARY, ART THOU LANGUID?

St. Matthew 11 : 28.

ART thou weary, art thou languid,
　　Art thou sore distrest?
"Come to Me," saith One, "and coming,
　Be at rest."

Hath He marks to lead me to Him,
　If He be my guide?
"In His feet and hands are wound-prints,
　And His side."

Is there diadem, as monarch,
   That His brow adorns?
"Yea, a crown, of very surety,
   But of thorns."

If I find Him, if I follow,
   What is guerdon here?
"Many a sorrow, many a labor,
   Many a tear."

If I still hold closely to Him,
   What hath He at last?
"Sorrow vanquished, labor ended,
   Jordan past."

If I ask Him to receive me,
   Will He say me nay?
"Not till earth, and not till heaven
   Pass away."

Finding, following, keeping, struggling,
   Is He sure to bless?
"Saints, Apostles, Prophets, Martyrs,
   Answer, Yes."

THE BORDER LAND.

I HAVE been to a land, a Border Land,
   Where there was but a strange, dim light;
Where shadows and dreams, in a spectral band
   Seem'd real to the aching sight.
I scarce bethought me how there I came,
   Or if thence I should pass again;
Its morning and night were mark'd by the flight,
   Or coming, of woe and pain.

But I saw from this land, this Border Land,
   With its mountain ridges hoar,
That they look'd across to a wondrous strand;
   A bright and unearthly shore.
Then I turned me to Him, "*the Crucified,*"
   In most humble faith and prayer,
Who had ransom'd with blood my sinful soul,
   For I thought He would call me there.

Yet nay: for awhile in the Border Land
   He bade me in patience stay,
And gather rich fruits with a trembling hand,
   Whilst He chased its glooms away;
He had led me amid those shadows dim,
   And shown that bright world so near,

To teach me that earnest trust in Him
  Is "the one thing needful" here.

And so far from the land, the Border Land,
  I have turned me to earth once more;
But earth and its works were such trifles, scann'd
  By the light of that radiant shore.
And oh! should they ever possess me again
  Too deeply, in heart and hand,
I must think how empty they seem'd, and vain,
  From the heights of the Border Land.

The Border Land hath depths and vales,
  Where sorrow for sin was known;
Where small seem'd great, as weigh'd in scales,
  Held by God's hand alone.
'Twas a land where earthly pride was naught,
  Where the poor were brought to mind,
With their scanty bed, their fireless cot,
  And their bread so hard to find.

But little I heard in the Border Land,
  Of all that passed below;
The once loud voices of human life
  To the deafened ear were low.
I was deaf to the clang of its trumpet call,
  And alike to its gibe or its sneer;

Its riches were dust, and the loss of all
  Would then scarce have cost a tear.

I met with a Friend in this Border Land,
  Whose teachings can come with power
To the blinded eye and the deafen'd ear,
  In affliction's loneliest hour.
"Times of refreshing" to the soul,
  In languor, oft he brings,
Prepares it then to meditate
  On high and glorious things.

Oh! Holy Ghost! too often grieved
  In health and earthly haste,
I bless those slow and silent hours
  Which seem'd to run to waste.
I would not *but* have pass'd those "depths,"
  And such communion known,
As can be held in the Border Land
  With Thee, and Thee alone.

I have been to a land, a Border Land!
  May oblivion never roll
O'er the mighty lessons which there and then
  Have been graven on my soul!
I have trodden a path I did not know,
  Safe in my Saviour's hand:
I can trust Him for all the future, now
  I have been to the Border Land.

LOVEST THOU ME?

DO I not love Thee? Thou whose patient feet
   Pressed Olivet's green slopes, or wearily,
Day after day, along the city's street,
      'Mid toil and heat,
   Bore the hard lot of our humanity?

Do I not love Thee? Thou who stood beside
   The sorrowing sisters, and gave back the life,
Dearer than life to them, nor yet denied,
      Oh, crucified!
   The Ruler's prayer, with love's keen anguish rife?

Whose gentle words of tenderest pity, drew
   Young children to Thine arms in fond embrace,
While benedictions sweet as evening dew—
      Ah! happy few—
   Fell on each shining head and upturned face?

Aye, in our mortal guise, my heart to Thee
   Turns with a love, which every thought o'erwhelms,
And calls Thee by that sweetest name to me,

Breathed reverently,
"Our elder brother, like unto ourselves."

I feel that I may love Thee as the Babe
  Of Bethlehem's manger, as the wondrous Boy
Among the temple doctors, strangely brave,
      As He who gave
The wine mysterious, 'mid the marriage joy—

In fisher boats upon Tiberias Sea,
  Or with Samaria's daughter at the well,
Feeding the multitudes who followed Thee,
      Or patiently
Teaching high truths in glowing parable.

But Thou art gone, the blue o'er-arching sky
  Hath hid Thee from our earnest upward gaze.
At God's right hand in peerless majesty
      Thou sitt'st eternally,
Enthroned supreme, through everlasting days.

Circled with light, by countless hosts adored;
  Back to those glorious realms in triumph led,
How can my puny love pursue the road
      Which saints have trod,
But where my weak affection fails to tread?

How, dazed and blinded, can I e'er attain

Those radiant heights of glories manifold?
My heart climbs after Thee in vain, in vain
    I still complain,—
Have pity, for my warmest love is cold.

Cold to the matchless love which paid for me
  A mighty ransom, won through shame and loss,—
The scourge, the crown, the garden's agony,
    The night of Calvary,
The dripping life-blood and the cruel cross!

O for a glance of Thy kind human face!
  Then might I love Thee as I long to do.
If its pure lineaments I could but trace
    One moment's space,
  Would not my vowed affection prove more true?

Would I not press, like Mary, to Thy feet,
  Who poured the perfumed oil with rev'rent touch?
And hear, perchance, Thy gracious lips repeat,
    In accents sweet,
  "Her sins are pardoned, for she loveth much."

She loveth much, O wandering heart of mine!
  When shall this blest assurance be Thine own?

Saviour, Redeemer, human yet Divine,
    Each throb be Thine,
And for my lack may Thy great love atone.

THE SYMPATHY OF JESUS.

Isaiah 32 : 18.

THERE is a secret place of rest
    God's saints alone may know;
Thou shalt not find it east nor west,
    Though seeking to and fro.
A cell where Jesus is the door,
    His love the only key:
Who enter will go out no more,
    But there with Jesus be.

If thou hadst dwelt within that place,
    Then would thine heart the while,
In vision of the Saviour's face,
    Forget all other smile;
Forget the charm earth's waters had,
    If once thy foot had trod
Beside the river that makes glad
    The city of our God.

If once such joy had filled thine heart,
    Earth's hatred, or earth's scorn,
Would seem but as a moment's smart,

Forgot as soon as borne.
Nay, thou in pain, or shame, or loss,
   Christ's fellowship would see,
And with thine heart embrace the cross
   On which He hung for thee.

Wouldst count it blest to live, to die,
   Where He is all in all:
Where rapt, earth unperceived goes by,
   And from ourselves we fall.
Till, from His secret place below,
   To mansions fair above,
He leads thee, there to make thee know
   The perfect joys of love.

OH, WEARY IN THE MORNING.

St. John 16:33.

OH, weary in the morning,
   When soft the dewdrops fall,
And weary at the noontide,
   When God's sun shines on all;
And weary at the nightfall,
   When, each day's labor o'er,
I count my misspent moments
   As lost for evermore.

OH, WEARY IN THE MORNING.

Oh, weary of the turmoil,
  The striving, and the care,
And weary of the burthen
  Which we of earth must bear;
Oh, weary of vain longings,
  And weary with vain fears,
And wearier with heart-sorrows
  Than with the weight of years.

Yet like a ray of sunlight,
  The Word shines through the gloom,
And after winter's darkness
  Comes spring in fresher bloom;
And after vainly searching,
  We find a resting meet;
For rest, and hope, and glory
  Are found at Jesus' feet.

God never sends a sorrow
  Without the healing balm,
And bids us fight no battles
  But for the victor's palm.
Yet we by earth's mist blinded,
  Knew not His holy will,
Till o'er the troubled waters
  His voice said, "Peace, be still!"

We will go forth and conquer,
  Depending on His grace;

The lowliest station near Him
    Must be an honored place!
And after battle, victory;
    And after victory, rest—
Like the beloved apostle,
    Upon the Master's breast!

GO NOT FAR FROM ME.

GO not far from me, O my strength,
    Whom all my times obey;
Take from me anything Thou wilt,
    But go not Thou away,—
And let the storm that does Thy work
    Deal with me as it may.

On Thy compassion I repose,
    In weakness and distress:
I will not ask for greater ease,
    Lest I should love Thee less.
Oh, 'tis a blessed thing for me
    To need Thy tenderness.

While many sympathizing hearts
    For my deliverance care,
Thou, in Thy wiser, stronger love,
    Art teaching me to bear—

By the sweet voice of thankful song,
    And calm, confiding prayer.

Thy love has many a lighted path, .
    No outward eye can trace,
And my heart sees Thee in the deep,
    With darkness on its face,
And communes with Thee, 'mid the storm,
    As in a secret place.

O comforter of God's redeemed,
    Whom the world does not see,
What hand should pluck me from the flood,
    That casts my soul on Thee?
Who would not suffer pain like mine,
    To be consoled like me?

When I am feeble as a child,
    And flesh and heart give way,
Then on Thy everlasting strength,
    With passive trust I stay.
And the rough wind becomes a song,
    The darkness shines like day.

Oh, blessed are the eyes that see,
    Through silent anguish show,
The love that in their hours of sleep,
    Unthanked may come and go.

And blessed are the ears that hear,
   Though kept awake by woe.

Happy are they that learn, in Thee,
   Though patient suffering teach,
The secret of enduring strength,
   And praise too deep for speech—
Peace that no pressure from without,
   No strife within, can reach.

There is no death for me to fear,
   For Christ, my Lord, hath died;
There is no curse in this my pain,
   For He was crucified.
And it is *fellowship* with Him
   That keeps me near His side.

My heart is fixed, O God, my strength—
   My heart is strong to bear;
I will be joyful in Thy love,
   And peaceful in Thy care.
Deal with me, for my Saviour's sake,
   According to His prayer.

No suffering while it lasts is joy,
   How blest soe'er it be—
Yet may the chastened child be glad
   His Father's face to see;

And oh, it is not hard to bear
   What must be borne in Thee.

It is not hard to bear by faith,
   In Thy own bosom laid,
The trial of a soul redeemed,
   For Thy rejoicing made.
Well may the heart in patience rest,
   That none can make afraid.

Safe in Thy sanctifying grace,
   Almighty to restore—
Borne onward—sin and death behind,
   And love and life before—
Oh, let my soul abound in hope,
   And praise Thee more and more!

Deep unto deep may call, but I
   With peaceful heart will say—
Thy loving-kindness hath a charge
   No waves can take away;
And let the storm that speeds me home,
   Deal with me as it may.

REST FROM THE BURDEN.

GOD sends sometimes a stillness in our life,
    The bivouac, the sleep,
When on the silent battle-field the strife
    Is hushed in slumber deep,
When wearied hearts exhausted sink to rest,
Remembering nor the struggle nor the quest.

We know such hours, when the dim dewy night
    Bids day's hot turmoil cease;
When star by star steals noiselessly in sight,
    With silent smiles of peace;
When we lay down our load, and half forget
The morrow comes, and we must bear it yet.

We know such hours, when after days of pain,
    And nights when sleep was not,
God gives us ease, and peace, and calm again,
    Till, all the past forgot,
We say, in rest and thankfulness most deep,
E'en so "He giveth His beloved sleep."

When some strong chain that bound us, by God's strength
    Is loosed or torn apart;
Or when, beloved and longed for, come at length,

REST FROM THE BURDEN.

Some friend makes glad our heart;
We know the calm that follows on such bliss,
That looks no farther, satisfied with this.

God does not always loose the chain, nor give
    The loved ones back to us;
Sometimes 'mid strife and tumult we must live,
    Learning His silence thus:
There is a rest for those who bear His will,
A peacefulness than freedom sweeter still.

He giveth rest, more perfect, pure, and true,
    While we His burthen bear;
It springeth not from parted pain, but through
    The accepted blessing there;
The lesson pondered o'er with thoughtful eyes,
The faith that sees in all a meaning wise.

Deep in the heart of pain God's hand hath set
    A hidden rest and bliss;
Take as His gift the pain, the gift brings yet
    A truer happiness:
God's voice speaks, through it all, the high behest
That bids His people enter into rest.

A PRAYER FOR REST IN SICKNESS.
Psalms 41:3.

LORD, a whole long day of pain
  Now at last is o'er!
Ah, how much we can sustain
  I have felt once more;
Felt how frail are all our powers,
  And how weak our trust;
If Thou help not, these dark hours
  Crush us to the dust.

Could I face the coming night
  If Thou wert not near?
Nay, without Thy love and might
  I must sink with fear:
Round me falls the evening gloom,
  Sights and sounds all cease,
But within this narrow room
  Night will bring no peace.

Other weary eyes may close,
  All things seek their sleep;
Hither comes no soft repose,
  I must wake and weep.
Come then, Jesus, o'er me bend,
  Give me strength to cope

With my pains, and gently send
   Thoughts of peace and hope.

Draw my weary heart away
   From this gloom and strife,
And these fever pains allay
   With the dew of life;
Thou canst calm the troubled mind;
   Thou its dread can still;
Teach me to be all resigned
   To my Father's will.

Then if I must wake and weep
   All the long night through,
Thou the watch with me wilt keep,
   Friend and Guardian true;
In the darkness Thou wilt speak
   Lovingly with me,
Though my heart may vainly seek
   Words to breathe to Thee.

Whereso'er my couch is made,
   In Thy hands I lie;
And to Thee alone for aid
   Turns my restless eye:
Let my prayer grow weary never,
   Strengthen Thou th' oppress'd,
In Thy shadow, Lord, for ever
   Let me gently rest.

HELPLESS.

LORD, I had planned to do Thee service true,
    To be more humbly watchful unto prayer,
More faithful in obedience to Thy word,
    More bent to put away all earthly care.

I thought of sad hearts comforted and healed,
    Of wanderers turned into the pleasant way,
Of little ones preserved from sinful snare,
    Of dark homes brightened with a heavenly ray;

Of time all consecrated to Thy will,
    Of strength spent gladly for Thee day by day,—
When suddenly the Heavenly mandate came,
    That I should give it all, at once, away.

Thy blessèd hand came forth, and laid me down,
    Turned every beating pulse to throbs of pain,
Hushed all my prayers into one feeble cry,
    Then bid me to believe that loss was gain.

And was it loss to have indulged such hopes?
    Nay, they were gifts, from out the inner shrine;

Garlands that I might hang about Thy Cross,
  Gems, to surrender at the call Divine.

As chiseled image unresisting lies
  In niche by its own sculptor's hand designed,
So to my unemployed and silent life
  Let me in quiet meekness be resigned.

If works of Faith, and labors sweet of Love,
  May not be mine, yet patient Hope can be
Within my heart, like a bright censer's fire,
  With incense of Thanksgiving mounting free.

Thou art our Pattern to the end of time,
  O Crucified! and perfect is Thy will;
The workers follow Thee in doing good,
  The helpless think of Calvary, and are still.

TEACH ME TO LIVE.

TEACH me to live! 'Tis easier far to die—
  Gently and silently pass away—
On earth's long night to close the heavy eye
  And waken in the glorious realms of day.

Teach me that harder lesson—how to live,
  To serve Thee in the darkest paths of life;
Arm me for conflict now, fresh vigor give,

And make me more than conqueror in the
    strife.

Teach me to live Thy purpose to fulfil:
    Bright for Thy glory let my taper shine:
Each day renew, remould this stubborn will;
    Closer round Thee my heart's affections
    twine.

Teach me to live for self and sin no more;
    But use the time remaining to me yet;
Not mine own pleasure seeking as before,
    Wasting no precious hours in vain regret.

Teach me to live, no idler let me be,
    But in Thy service hand and heart employ,
Prepared to do Thy bidding cheerfully—
    Be this my highest and my holiest joy.

Teach me to live—my daily cross to bear,
    Nor murmur though I bend beneath its load,
Only be with me; let me feel Thee near,
    Thy smile sheds gladness on the darkest road.

Teach me to live and find my life in Thee,
    Looking from earth and earthly things away.
Let me not falter, but untiringly
    Press on, and gain new strength and power
    each day.

Teach me to live! With kindly words for all,
  Wearing no cold, repulsive brow of gloom,
Waiting with cheerful patience till Thy call
  Summons my spirit to her heavenly home.

NOT NOW.

NOT *now*, my child,—a little more rough tossing,
  A little longer on the billow's foam,
A few more journeyings in the desert darkness,
  And then the sunshine of Thy Father's home.

Not *now*, for I have wanderers in the distance,
  And thou must call them in with patient love;
Not *now*, for I have sheep upon the mountains,
  And thou must follow them where'er they rove.

Not *now*, for I have loved ones, sad and weary,
  Wilt thou not cheer them with a kindly smile?
Sick ones who need thee in their lonely sorrow,
  Wilt thou not tend them yet a little while?

Not *now*, for wounded hearts are sorely bleeding,

And thou must teach those widowed hearts
    to sing;
Not *now*, for orphans' tears are thickly falling,
    They must be gathered 'neath some shelter-
        ing wing.

Not *now*, for many a hungry one is pining,
    Thy willing hand must be outstretched and
        free;
Thy Father hears the mighty cry of anguish,
    And gives His answering messages to thee.

Not *now*, for hell's eternal gulf is yawning,
    And souls are perishing in hopeless sin;
Jerusalem's bright gates are standing open,—
    Go to the banished ones and bring them in.

Go with the name of Jesus to the dying,
    And speak that name in all its living power;
Why should thy fainting heart grow chill and
        weary,
    Canst thou not "watch with Me one little
        hour?"

One little hour, and then the glorious crowning,
    The golden harp-strings and the victor's
        palm;—
One little hour, and then the Alleluia,
    Eternity's long, deep, thanksgiving psalm!

THE BLESSED HEALER.

Psalms 138: 7.

WHEN across the heart, deep waves of sorrow
　Break, as on a dry and barren shore;
When hope glistens with no bright to-morrow,
　And the storm seems sweeping evermore.

When the cup of every earthly gladness
　Bears no taste of the life-giving stream;
And high hopes, as though to mock our sadness,
　Fade and die as in some fitful dream:

Who shall hush the weary spirit's chiding?
　Who the aching void within shall fill?
Who shall whisper of a peace abiding,
　And each surging billow calmly still?

Only He whose wounded heart was broken
　With the bitter cross and thorny crown;
Whose dear love glad words of joy had spoken,
　Who His life for us laid meekly down.

Blessed Healer! all our burdens lighten;
　Give us peace, Thine own sweet peace, we pray;
Keep us near Thee till the morn shall brighten,
　And all mists and shadows flee away!

BY THEE, JESUS, WILL I STAY.

St. Matthew 28 : 20.

BY Thee, Jesus, will I stay,
   Evermore Thy servant stand;
From Thee my feet shall never stray,
   But I will go where points Thy hand.

Thou! life of all the life that's mine,
   My soul's sore-sap and vital power.
As to its branch, from out the vine,
   Flows sap of life from hour to hour.

Stay near me through this heat and glow,
   Stay near, too, when my day sinks down,
And long the evening shadows grow,
   And the night comes stealing on.

Lay in blessing, then, Thy hand
   On my weary, weakly head;
Saying, "Rest, child! to the land
   Thy faith hath sought thou shalt be led."

Stay near me; in Thine arms enfold,
   When most the chill of death I dread;
Chill, like the sharp and bitter cold,
   Ere dawns in Heaven the morning red.

When darkness shall mine eyes o'ertake,
   Light Thou my spirit through the gloom,
That unto me the morn may break
   As breaks to him the exile's home.

PEACEABLE FRUIT.

"Never the less afterward it yieldeth the peaceable fruit of righteousness." Hebrews 12 : 11.

WHAT shall Thine "afterward" be, O Lord,
   For this dark and suffering night?
Father, what shall Thine "afterward" be?
Hast Thou a morning joy for me,
   And a new and joyous light?

What shall Thine "afterward" be, O Lord,
   For the moan that I can not stay?
Wilt Thou turn it to some new song of praise,
Sweeter than sorrowless heart could raise,
   When the night hath passed away?

What shall Thine "afterward" be, O Lord,
   For this helplessness of pain?
A clearer view of my home above,
Of my Father's strength and my Father's love?
   Shall this be my lasting gain?

What shall Thine "afterward" be, O Lord,
   How long must Thy child endure?
Thou knowest! 'tis well that I know it not!
Thine "afterward" cometh; I can not tell what,
   But I know that Thy word is sure.

What shall Thine "afterward" be, O Lord?
   I wonder and wait to see;
(While to Thy chastening hand I bow)
What "peaceable fruit" may be ripening now,
   Ripening fast for me?

REST IN GOD.

UNDER the shadow of Thy wings, my Father,
   'Til these calamities be over past!
In that sure refuge let my spirit gather
   Strength to look calmly back upon the past.

Be merciful to me! for thoughts that crush me
   Lie like a weight of sorrow on my breast;
Only Thy voice, Omnipotent, can hush me
   Into the quiet e'en of seeming rest.

Thou knowest—Thou only—the dark chain that binds me,
   The heavy chain which eats into my soul;

The links of adamant which have entombed me,
  Binding each feeling in their chill control.

Oh! what is life but one long, long endurance,
  Of this dull, heavy weight on heart and brain?
Speak to my spirit—speak the strong assurance
  That nothing Thou ordainest is in vain.

Trembling amid the turmoils of existence,
  Oh! let me grasp a more than mortal arm;
Father! my Father! be not at a distance
  When earth's dark phantoms Thy weak child alarm.

Under Thy shadow! Fear cannot appall me,
  If in the Rock of Ages surely hid.
Under Thy shadow! Harm cannot befall me
  If Thou—All-wise! All-merciful!—forbid.

Nearer to Thee! my Saviour! my Redeemer!
  In earth, or heaven, whom hath my soul but Thee?
Though for an instant, as some feverish dreamer
  Grasps at the treasures which he seems to see,

I, too, have dreamed, and waked to find "illusion"
  Inscribed on all I sought to make my own,

And turning from my idols in confusion,
  I dedicate my life to Thee alone.

Under the shadow of Thy wing abiding,
  Close to a sympathizing Saviour's side,
In the sure promise of His love confiding,
  Why should I shrink, though earthly ills betide

Oh! if the soul grew strong through suffering only,
  If but through trial it may reach its goal,
I will rejoice, although my way be lonely,
  And all Thy waves and billows o'er me roll.

Yes! I will praise Thee! though my tears are falling
  Upon the trembling harp-string as I sing;
Am I not safe—though grief my soul is thralling—
  Under the shadow of my Father's wing?

"HE CARETH FOR YOU."

IF I could only surely know
  That all these things that tire me so
  Were noticed by my Lord.
The pang that cuts me like a knife,

The lesser pains of daily life,
The noise, the weariness, the strife,
    What peace it would afford!

I wonder if He really shares
In all my little human cares,
    This mighty King of kings.
If He who guides each blazing star
Through realms of boundless space afar
Without confusion, sound, or jar,
    Stoops to these petty things.

It seems to me, if sure of this,
Blent with each ill would come such bliss,
    That I might covet pain,
And deem whatever brought to me
The loving thought of Deity,
And sense of Christ's sweet sympathy,
    No loss, but richest gain.

Dear Lord, my heart hath not a doubt
That Thou dost compass me about
    With sympathy Divine.
The love for me once crucified
Is not a love to leave my side,
But waiteth ever to divide
    Each smallest care of mine.

THE FISHER.

SORROW, and strife, and pain
    Have crushed my spirit with relentless hand,
Long have I toiled, O Lord, and wrought in vain,
    But still at Thy command,

Into the wide blue sea,
    Clinging to Thine own word, I cast the net;
The covenant was made of old with me,
    And I will trust Thee yet.

Lord, it is hard to stand
    Waiting and watching in this silent toil,
While other fishers draw their nets to land,
    And shout to see their spoil.

My strength fails unawares,
    My hands are weak,—my sight grows dim with tears;
My soul is burdened with unanswered prayers,
    And sick of doubts and fears.

I see across the deep,
    The moon cast down her fetters, silver-bright,

As if to bind the ocean in his sleep
  With links of living light.

I hear the roll and rush
  Of waves that kiss the bosom of the beach;
That soft sea-voice which ever seems to hush
  The tones of human speech.

A breeze comes sweet and chill
  Over the waters, and the night wanes fast;
His promise fails; the net is empty still,
  And hope's old dreams are past!

Slow fade the moon and stars,
  And in the east the new dawn faintly shines
Through dim, grey shadows, flecked with pearly
    bars,
  And level silver lines.

But lo! what form is this
  Standing beside me on the desolate shore?
I bow my knees; His garment's hem I kiss;
  Master, I doubt no more!

"Draw in thy net, draw in,"
  He cries, "behold the straining meshes
    break!"
Ah, Lord, the spoil I toiled so long to win
  Is granted for Thy sake!

The rosy day blooms out
  Like a full-blossomed flower; the joyous sea
Lifts up its voice; the winds of morning shout
  All glory, God, to Thee!

SOME TIME.

SOME time, when all life's lessons have been
    learned,
  And suns and stars for evermore have set,
The things which our weak judgments here
    have spurned,
  The things o'er which we grieved with lashes
    wet,
Will flash before us, and life's dark night,
  As stars shine most in deeper tints of blue;
And we shall see how all God's plans were
    right,
  And what most seemed reproof was love
    most true:

And we shall see how, while we frown and sigh,
  God's plans go on as best for you and me—
How, when we called, He heeded not our cry,
  Because His wisdom to the end could see;
And e'en as prudent parents disallow
  Too much of sweet to craving babyhood,

So God, perhaps, is keeping from us now
   Life's sweetest things because it seemeth
      good.

And if, sometimes, commingled with life's wine,
   We find the wormwood, and rebel and shrink,
Be sure a wiser hand than yours or mine
   Pours out this potion for our lips to drink;
And if some friend we love is lying low,
   Where human kisses cannot reach his face,
Oh, do not blame the loving Father so,
   But wear your sorrow with obedient grace!

And you shall shortly know that lengthened
      breath
   Is not the sweetest gift God sends His friend,
And that sometimes the sable pall of death
   Conceals the fairest boon His love can send;
If we could push ajar the gates of life,
   And stand within, and all God's working see,
We could interpret all this doubt and strife,
   And for each mystery could find a key.

But not to-day. Then be content, poor heart!
   God's plans, like lilies, pure and white unfold;
We must not tear the close-shut leaves apart,
   Time will reveal the Calyxes of gold;
And if, through patient toil, we reach the land

Where tired feet with sandals loosed may rest,
Where we shall clearly know and understand,
  I think that we will say, "God knew the best."

LEAD THOU ME ON.

O LEAD me on; the way is dark without
    Thee,
Thou great Redeemer from all sin and woe;
Amid life's changes may I never doubt Thee,
  But follow still where Thou dost bid me go.

Lead Thou me on, Guide of the weak and
    dreary;
  Be Thou my help when thorny is the way;
Without Thy smile my heart is sad and weary,
  But hope immortal brightens in its ray.

Lead Thou me on while storms of life o'ertake
    me;
  Then may Thy promise on my spirit fall,
"Lo! I am with thee," "I will not forsake
    thee,"
  With heaven-born music 'mid the gloomy
    thrall.

Lead Thou me on in hours of fierce temptation;
  Then may I triumph through the blood divine;

Then may I know the power of Thy salvation,
  And in the likeness of Thy glory shine.

Lead Thou me on; there is no guide beside
    Thee—
  No sure, unfailing beacons but Thine own;
If Thou art nigh, whatever may betide me
  Will only draw me nearer to the throne.

Lead Thou me on; too long my soul has
    doubted;
  "Come unto Me," I hear Thee sweetly say;
Too long cold unbelief my path has shrouded;
  Forgive me, Saviour; hear me while I pray.

Lead Thou me, O Man of Sorrows, ever,
  Thou who didst bear our own upon the tree;
Grant me Thy peace; and may it, like a river,
  Flow through my heart from love's unbounded
    sea.

Oh, lead me on till I have gained the river
  Whose surges break on the eternal strand:
Then guide my spirit to the bright forever,
  Through golden portals to the sinless land.

A PRESENT SAVIOUR.

WE sometimes think that had our lot been cast
   Upon the earth when Jesus labored here,
We would have sought Him with a joyful haste
   To breathe our troubles in His listening ear.

We think that over many a weary league
   We would have gladly toiled our Lord to meet,
Unmindful of the danger and fatigue,
   Could we at last but worship at His feet.

We think that they were blest above their kind
   Who saw Him as He went from place to place,
While we, less fortunate, our Lord must find
   Through the mysterious workings of His grace.

Alas! how prone to murmur and repine!
   How prone we are to count our blessings less!
How, like the doubting Jews, we seek a sign,
   And daily slight His precious promises!

For we forget the priceless words He left,
  "Lo, I am with you alway—to the end,"
And that, though by all other friends bereft,
  He ever stands near by a constant friend.

More blest than they of old Jerusalem,
  We can, where'er on earth we are the while,
But reach our hands to touch His garment's hem,
  But look, to greet His ever-pardoning smile.

"KEEP ME FROM FALLING!"

"KEEP me from falling!"
  O Lamb of God, whose ever-pitying eye
Looks down from Heaven at each disciple's cry,
I come, a suppliant, needing all Thy care,
And in my joys and griefs repeat this prayer,
  "Keep me from falling!"

"Keep me from falling!"
If in the darkness I should stray afar,
Like some lost traveler, with no guiding star,
Be Thou my Light, O Jesus, Thou my Friend,
And o'er these stony paths to life's dark end,
  "Keep me from falling!"

>   "Keep me from falling!"
> When I am tempted by the world to sin,
> Let Love Divine make pure my heart within;—
> Press nearer Lord;—be constant at my side,—
> Hear Thou my cry;—yea, with me still abide,
>   "Keep me from falling!"
>
>   "Keep me from falling!"
> Soon shall I tread the shores of that dark sea,
> Which all my hopes, my fears divide from Thee;
> Then, Saviour, help me, shrinking from Death's tide,—
> Stretch out Thy hand my tottering feet to guide,
>   "Keep me from falling!"

A SONG OF ABEL IN HEAVEN.

> TEN thousand times ten thousand sung
>   Loud anthems round the throne,
> When lo! one solitary tongue
>   Began a song unknown;
> A song unknown to angel ears,
> A song that told of banished fears,
> Of pardoned sins and dried-up tears.
>
> Not one of all the heavenly host
>   Could these high notes attain,
> But spirits from a distant coast

United in the strain;
Till he who first began the song,
To sing alone not suffered long,
Was mingled with a countless throng.

And still, as hours are fleeting by,
    The angels ever bear
Some newly ransomed soul on high,
    To join the chorus there.
And so the song will louder grow,
Till all redeemed by Christ below
To that fair world of rapture go.

O give me, Lord, my golden harp,
    And tune my broken voice,
That I may sing of troubles sharp,
    Exchanged for endless joys;
The song that ne'er was heard before,
A sinner reached the heavenly shore,
But now shall sound forevermore.

WHEN THE KING COMES IN!

Matthew xxii. 11-14.

BROTHER, called by Christ's name are we!
    Sitting, too, where His people be,
But how will it fare with thee and me,
    When the King comes in?

Crowns on the head where thorns have been!
Glorified, He who once died for men!
Splendid the vision before us then,
      When the King comes in!

Then will His eye scan every guest,
Reading the secrets of every breast;
Ah! well for us if we stand the test
      When the King comes in!

Like lightning's flash will that instant show
Things long hidden from friend and foe;
Just what we are, will each neighbor know
      When the King comes in!

Then will He see if every one
Has the wedding-garment of true faith on;
They who have not will be all undone,
      When the King comes in!

Too late to secure it in that day,
Vainly they'll hide from Him away—
Condemned, rejected, outcast, they,
      When the King comes in!

Endless the separations then!
Bitter the cries of deluded men!
Awful that moment, beyond all ken,
      When the King comes in!

Then may we sit with those who are called,
By holy rite and ordinance walled,
And yet at the end be startled, appalled,
  When the King comes in !

Friend ! be sure that thou be such guest
That on thee with joy His eye may rest,
And thou chosen be for the feast of the Blest,
  When the King comes in !

Lord ! grant us all, we implore Thee, grace,
So to await Thee, each in his place,
That we will not tremble to see Thy face
  When Thou comest in !

"GIVE US THIS DAY OUR DAILY BREAD."

ONLY to-day ! dark looms to-morrow—
 Behind, sad yesterdays are lying dead ;
Each moment keeps slow step with sorrow ;
 Give us *to-day* our daily bread,—
  Only to-day!

We have no strength to walk, unless Thou lead
  us ;
 Sin hides, each side, the straight and narrow
  way ;

Our hungry souls must faint, except Thou feed
    us;
  Help us, we plead, to live aright to-day,—
    Only to-day!

We would not pierce the misty clouds around us,
  Nor fathom what the future has in store;
But day by day Thy loving care hath found us:
  Lead us to-day, we ask no more,—
    Only to-day!

We could not bear the weight a lifetime carries;
  Our strength grows weakness if we do but
    try;
To-morrow comes with pace that never tarries;
  Help us to-day, O Lord, is all our cry,—
    Only to-day!

STRIFE AND VICTORY.

THERE came an angel to me in disguise,
  Whose name was Sorrow: tender were
    His eyes,
      Though harsh His hand;
And slowly my reluctant soul He led
Within the hearing of a Voice which said,
    In sweet command:
"Come unto Me, and I will give you rest."

How could I but obey the kind behest?
   And, as I turned,
Some door of Heaven unbarred to flood my way
With glimpses of the everlasting day,
   Such glory burned;
Then in my gladness, "This is peace!" I said;
But Life replied, ere many days had sped,
   "Not peace, but hope!"
For, while I looked, the transient gleam was gone,
As clouds across the rift are drifted on,
   In heaven's dark cope.

Ah, then I felt the galling chains of sin!
Ah, then I found that peace is hard to win
   With such a foe!
But as I strove with evil, strength was given,
And still my steady feet were turned toward Heaven,
   Though faint and slow.

And thus I struggled on from day to day,
Until I felt the hostile hosts give way,
   The pressure yield;
And then I knew a victory was won,
And I had conquered peace at last, upon
   Life's battle-field.

Not that the strife was wholly ended yet,
Nor triumph perfect. Death alone can set
      On mortal brow
The victor's radiant crown ; yet peace within
Is won by conquest over self and sin,
      Even here and now.

"Is it not then," you ask, "the gift of Christ,
His precious legacy, unearned, unpriced?"
      Yes, this we know ;
But Christ's best gifts are not for him who stands
Awaiting them with idle, outstretched hands.
      He gives not so.

He bought for us a field whereon to stand,
And fight life's battle under His command,
      With woe and sin :
He paid His life with power to help, and thus
His gift is that 'tis possible for us
      To strive and win.

For when we strive, we win. Oh, blest be He
Who always giveth us the victory
      In faithful strife,
And crowns the conquest with His holy peace,
Whose early beams grow brighter and increase
      To endless life !

MY COMFORTER.

SERENE I lie in Jesus' hands,
   Without one anxious care;
Content to do what He commands,
   And what He wills, to bear.

Just now the cup He bids me drink,
   Like Marah's water seems;
And all the active scenes of life
   Come to me but in dreams.

Yet as I lie so faint, so weak,
   I feel that He can be
A precious help in time of need,
   And Comforter to me.

So calmly, peacefully, I lean
   Upon my Saviour's breast;
For if He sends me life, or death,
   Whate'er He gives is best.

ONE STEP MORE.

WHAT though before me it is dark,
   Too dark for me to see?
I ask but light for one step more;
   'Tis quite enough for me.

ONE STEP MORE.

Each little humble step I take,
    The gloom clears from the next;
So, though 'tis very dark beyond,
    I never am perplexed.

And if sometimes the mist hangs close,
    So close I fear to stray,
Patient I wait a little while,
    And soon it clears away.

I would not see my further path,
    For mercy veils it so;
My present steps might harder be
    Did I the future know.

It may be that my path is rough,
    Thorny, and hard, and steep;
And, knowing this, my strength might fail
    Through fear and terror deep.

It may be that it winds along
    A smooth and flowery way;
But seeing this, I might despise
    The journey of to-day.

Perhaps my path is very short,
    My journey nearly done;
And I might tremble at the thought
    Of ending it so soon.

Or, if I saw a weary length
   Of road that I must wend,
Fainting, I'd think, "My feeble powers
   Will fail me ere the end."

And so I do not wish to see
   My journey o'er its length;
Assured that, through my Father's love,
   Each step will bring its strength.

Thus step by step I onward go,
   Not looking far before;
Trusting that I shall always have
   Light for just "one step more."

A LITTLE WHILE.

MY silence and my solitude
   I offer up to Thee.
Lord, where the glad Hosannas sound,
   Wilt Thou not think of me?

Oh, many the foundations are
   Of Thy fair City tall,
And many are the gates of Pearl
   Set in the Jasper wall.

And many are the Mansions there,
    And many are the feet,
Upon the jewelled pavements, where
    The saved and happy meet.

A little while, and shall I be
    One of that radiant throng?
A little while, and shall I join
    Their everlasting song?

A little while,—O throbbing heart,
    Then surely Thou canst wait
A little while, and learn to be
    Serene though desolate.

A PROTEST.

WHY press we so against the door that Fate
    Has barred upon our heart's desire?
Why hold our lives bereft and desolate
    Because God writes their almanac in fire?
Why should we sadden with dark, clouded skies,
    When others make a ladder of their love;
And while we deem ourselves too weak to rise,
    They've climbed above?

Why sit and dream in Spring's sweet labor time,

Unreal dreams, whose sadness makes them
   sweet ;
And, since we mar and break our lives full
   prime,
Deem that we rest contented at God's feet ?
Why cry to heaven for lost and broken hours,
   For faith and hope that faded long ago,
When still within our hearts new fruitful powers
   Are budding now ?

Oh, eyes turned inward on our darkened hearts
   Open to see God's beauty on the earth,
Self-pitying tears that flow upon His smarts,
   Fructify all our barrenness and dearth :
O folded hands, close-clasped in dull despair,
   Grow busy with God's work of love and peace,
O heart, forget to grieve, and rise to where
   Misgivings cease.

"CONFORMITY TO CHRIST."

LORD, I desire to live as one
   That bears a blood-bought name ;
As one who fears but grieving Thee,
   And knows no other shame.

As one by whom Thy life below
   Should never be forgot ;

"CONFORMITY TO CHRIST."

    As one who fain would live apart
        From those that love Thee not.

    I want to be as one who knows
        Thy fellowship of love ;
    As one whose eyes can pierce beyond
        The pearl-built gates above.

    As one who daily speaks to Thee,
        And hears Thy voice Divine,
    With depths of tenderness declare,
        "Beloved, thou art mine."

    I want to walk as one who knows
        The guilt that lurks within ;
    Yet rests in meek dependence
        On the resting-place from sin.

    Nearer my Saviour's face to dwell
        Than ever yet before ;
    And then, to lean upon His breast,
        And own Him conqueror.

CHASTISEMENT.

I HAVE been dumb, and held my peace,
    Because the stroke was Thine:
When Thou dost bare Thy holy arm
    Omnipotent, Divine,
Shall mortal man, corrupt within,
Complain that Thou dost visit sin?

    Thou didst it, Lord. This sorrow came,
        Obedient to Thy will:
    Thy hands have made me; Oh, in wrath
        Remember mercy still.
I will be silent at Thy awful throne;
Lord, Thou hast fashion'd me: Thy will be done.

    Thou didst it. Thou whose heart of love
        Was wounded first for me:
    Who passed through mortal life, and bore
        Death's deepest agony.
How can I murmur or complain,
When Jesus suffered grief and pain?

    Thou didst it; who art watching now
        Each pang and heavy sigh:
    Yes, I submit, if only Thou
        Wilt hold me, and stand nigh:

I will not struggle with the knife
That wounds me but to save my life.

   Thou didst it, who art gone on high,
     Where many mansions be,
   There to prepare a glorious Home,
     And deathless friends for me:
Shall I rebel against the love
That fits me for my home above?

   Ah, no! e'en through this load of fears
     My heart is springing up
   To thank Thee for the boundless grace
     That overflows my cup.
But I am weak, and cannot always say,
"Thy will be done;" remember I am clay.

   Put a new song within my lips,
     And let my spirit sing;
   I give Thee up my inmost heart,
     Saviour, and Priest, and King;
Take to Thee, there at least, Thy power and
     reign;
Henceforth "to live is Christ, to die is gain."

ALPHA AND OMEGA.

O LAMB of God, I know that Thou art here!
Close as my clasping hands—nay, yet more near;
And every sigh enters Thy gracious ear,—
   I ask to see
More of Thyself, Lord Jesus, more of Thee!

Give me to walk with girded garments white;
The understanding heart, to read aright
Thy word, Thy Law, Thy will, my soul's delight,—
   That I may be
More like Thyself, Lord Jesus, more like Thee!

Grant me a ministry that Thou shalt bless.
Give me Thy comfort for the comfortless,
And self-forgetful in each heart's distress,—
   Oh, grant to me
More of Thyself, Lord Jesus, more of Thee!

Give me a baptism of glowing love,
Thy power and presence wheresoe'er I rove;
And my last prayer, all other prayers above,—
   Oh, give to me
More of Thyself, Lord Jesus, more of Thee!

REST.

O JESUS Merciful! bend down
   In Thy compassions deep,
As sleepless and alone I lie,
   And watch beside me keep.

There is a holier, sweeter rest
   Than the lulling of this pain;
And a deeper calm than that which sleep
   Sheds over heart and brain.

It is the soul's surrendered choice,
   The settling of the Will,
Lying down gently on the Cross,
   God's purpose to fulfill.

For this I need Thy Presence, Lord,
   My hand held close in Thine:[*]
Infuse now through my spirit faint
   An energy divine.

Feed me with Love, imprint on me
   Thine awful kiss of Peace:
Let me be still upon Thy Breast,
   Nor struggle for release.

---

[*] Isaiah xli. 13.

And sanctify my weakness, Lord;
   Nature's extreme distress,
Is just the time when it may learn
   God's glory to express.

Stamp in, O God, at any cost
   The likeness of Thy Son:
Filial submission to Thy will
   Is heaven itself begun.

MINE EYES SHALL SEE THEE.
Isaiah xxxiii. 17.

MINE eyes shall see Thee, O my Friend, my Sov'reign,
   Dear Lord of life and grace!
These very eyes, bedimm'd with woe and watching,
   Shall gaze upon Thy face!

Mine eyes, that now but see in part, and darkly,
   And but in part have known,
Shall face to face, yet fearlessly, behold Thee,
   O Lamb, upon Thy throne!

Mine eyes shall see Thee, not as once they saw Thee,

Who walked with Thee of old,
Yet knew Thee not, but in Thy perfect beauty
   I shall Thy face behold !

Light of my life ! O sweet and fair Lord Jesus,
   Joy of my inmost heart ;
What tongue can tell, what mind conceive the rapture
   To see Thee as Thou art ?

O matchless King ! my own, my only Saviour !
   My Royal, Princely One !
When shall these eyes, these wistful eyes be gladdened,
   And filled with Thee alone ?

Hasten, O Lord, Thy feet upon the mountains,
   Let the cold shadows flee !
This midnight watching must be well-nigh over
   That I have kept for Thee.

Soon shall the morning dawn upon my vigil,
   For, daybreak must be near ;
When in the glory of His likeness waking,
   With Christ I shall appear.

Mine eyes shall see Him ! then this tongue unloosened

Her new-born song shall sing;
That now half-trembling, half-triumphant falters
  "*Mine* eyes shall see the King."

THE BELEAGUERED SOUL.
ROMANS viii. 37.

BESET with foes, like some beleaguered city,
  My trembling soul amid the tumult stands,
Crying, "Look down, O Christ, in helpful pity
  Increase my faith, lift up my failing hands."

Thee will I love with all my soul's endeavor,
  Thee only serve, in spite of every foe;
I am Thy chosen one, Thine own for ever,
  And Thou art mine, 'mid conflict, toil, and woe.

Hast Thou not sworn in covenant unfailing
  That Thou wilt leave me never, or forsake;
And shall my feeblest cry be unavailing?
  Nay, Thou wilt front the battle for my sake.

Lo! while without mine enemies surround me,
  This traitor heart, leagued with the hosts of hell,

Cast wide her gates—but Thou whose love has found me,
    Wilt guard the camp, and keep the citadel.

Thou of the blood-stained vesture, O Victorious!
    With burning eyes, and many crownèd head;
Thou conquering One, with name unknown but glorious,
    Thou, Thou art He that liveth and was dead.

Thou art *that* Jesus, who, with footsteps lowly,
    Trod, stranger-wise, the busy haunts of earth;
Yet whose high deeds, and language pure and holy
    Proclaimed to sinful man Thy sinless birth.

Thou art that Jesus, who, despised and hooted,
    Shrank in meek anguish, 'neath the Father's rod;
The crucified, thorn-crowned, and persecuted,
    The Man of Sorrows, yet the Son of God!

Thou bleeding Lamb! Thou King of kings transcendent,
    Who, dying, death destroyed, his bondage rent;
Then rising, left the gloomy grave resplendent
    With faith, and hope, and love omnipotent.

O human-hearted Friend! O Prince eternal!
  Since Thy dear light hath dawn'd upon my heart,
Take all life's fresh springs, all her pastures vernal,
  For Thou my only joy shalt be and art.

"COMFORTABLE WORDS."

"Search the Scriptures: for in them ye think ye have eternal life: and they are they which testify of Me."— JOHN v. 39.

ART thou worn and heavy-laden,
  By earth's trials sore oppressed?
Hearken to thy Saviour's promise,
  "Come, and I will give thee rest;"
Lighter far would seem thy sorrows
  Did ye heed His blessed Word,
And, not faithless, but believing,
  "Cast thy burden on the Lord."

Though the way seem long and weary
  Earthly aid removed from thee,
Christ has promised—"As thy day is,
  Even so thy strength shall be."
Over paths most rough and stony,
  He will hold thy footsteps up,

And in sore and grievous trouble,
   Help thee drink the bitter cup.

Is a loved one taken from thee,
   Murmur not beneath the rod,
Know'st thou not that those most chastened
   Are the best beloved of God?
Though thy heart be sore and bleeding,
   From thy treasure called to part,
Comes there not to thee this message—
   "I am nigh the broken heart?"

"Where thy treasure, there thy heart is,"
   And whene'er disposed to roam,
'Tis the love you bore that dear one,
   Draws thy wand'ring footsteps Home.
This the thought that cheers thy sorrow
   When thine eyes with tears are dim,
Though "to me he shall return not,
   I may some time go to him."

Through still deeper waves of trouble
   God may call thee yet to go,
'Tis to draw thee closer to Him,
   Wean thy thoughts from things below.
Harden not thy heart against Him,
   Never doubt His care for thee,
"Greater love than this has no man,
   That He gave His life for thee."

Though thy griefs should nigh o'erwhelm thee,
   Each one seem more bitter still,
Strive for grace to say most humbly,
   "Lo! I come to do Thy will."
God shall be forever with thee,
   Help thee tread the narrow way,
And through deepest, blackest darkness,
   Guide thee to His perfect day.

Then, thy journey safely ended,
   From all fears thy soul set free,
Thou shalt, in thy Father's mansion,
   Find a place prepared for thee—
No more death, nor pain, nor sorrow,
   Never more from Home to stray,
God shall dry thy tears, and tell thee
   Former things are passed away.

There with angels and archangels
   Will ye laud His glorious name,
Saying, Holy, Holy, Holy,
   Ever through all time the same.
Would ye mourn o'er earthly trials,
   Be by troubles so oppressed,
Were ye looking ever upward,
   Toward that Home of perfect Rest?

"THOU ART NEAR, O LORD!"

WHEN the world is brightest,
And our hearts are lightest,
Blessèd Jesus, hear us!
Let Thy hand be near us!

When life's scene is shaded,
All its bright hopes faded,
Blessèd Jesus, hear us!
Light of heaven, be near us!

When with blessings sated
Or by praise elated,
Blessèd Jesus, hear us!
Let Thy Cross be near us!

When the night of sorrow
Makes us dread to-morrow,
Blessèd Jesus, hear us!
Light of heaven, be near us!

When our foes surround us!
When our sins have bound us,
Blessèd Jesus, hear us!
Let Thy help be near us!

When our hearts are grieving,
O'er the grave bereaving,
Blessèd Jesus, hear us!
Light of heaven, be near us!

When in sickness lying,
Dark with fear of dying,
Blessèd Jesus, hear us!
Let Thy help be near us!

When life, slowly waning,
Shows but Heaven remaining,
Blessèd Jesus, hear us!
Light of all, be near us!

THE STRAIGHT WAY.

"Make Thy way straight before my face."—Ps. v. 8.

THY way, not mine, O Lord,
   However dark it be!
Lead me by Thine own hand,
   Choose out the path for me.

Smooth let it be, or rough,
   It will be still the best;
Winding or straight, it leads
   Right onward to Thy Rest.

I dare not choose my lot ;
　　I would not if I might ;
Choose Thou for me, my God ;
　　So shall I walk aright.

The Kingdom that I seek
　　Is Thine ; so let the way
That leads to it be Thine,
　　Else I must surely stray.

Take Thou my cup, and it
　　With joy or sorrow fill,
As best to Thee may seem.
　　Choose Thou my good and ill.

Choose Thou for me my friends,
　　My sickness or my health ;
Choose Thou my cares for me,
　　My poverty or wealth.

Not mine, not mine the choice,
　　In things, or great, or small ;
Be Thou my Guide, my Strength,
　　My Wisdom, and my all.

OUR FATHER KNOWETH.

"Your Father knoweth that ye have need of these things."—ST. LUKE xii. 30.

THEREFORE, our Heavenly Father,
    We will not fear to pray
For the little needs and longings,
    That fill our every day;
And when we dare not whisper
    A want that lieth dim,
We say, "Our Father knoweth,"
    And leave it all to Him.

For His great love has compassed
    Our nature, and our need
We know not; but He knoweth,
    And He will bless indeed.
Therefore, O Heavenly Father,
    Give what is best to me;
And take the wants unanswered,
    As offerings made to Thee.

I WILL FOLLOW THEE.

O JESUS, I have promised
    To serve Thee to the end;
Be Thou for ever near me,
    My Master and My Friend!

I shall not fear the battle
  If Thou art by my side,
Nor wander from the pathway
  If Thou wilt be my Guide.

Oh! let me feel Thee near me—
  The world is ever near;
I see the sights that dazzle,
  The tempting sounds I hear.
My foes are ever near me,
  Around me and within;
But, Jesus, draw Thou nearer,
  And shield my soul from sin.

Oh! let me hear Thee speaking
  In accents clear and still,
Above the storms of passion,
  The murmurs of self-will.
Oh! speak to re-assure me,
  To hasten or control:
Oh! speak, and make me listen,
  Thou Guardian of my soul!

O Jesus, Thou hast promised
  To all that follow Thee
That where Thou art in glory
  There shall Thy servant be;
And, Jesus, I have promised

To serve Thee to the end;
Oh, give me grace to follow
　My Master and my Friend!

Oh! let me see Thy foot-marks,
　And in them plant mine own;
My hope to follow duly
　Is in Thy strength alone.
Oh! guide me, call me, draw me,
　Uphold me to the end;
And then in heaven receive me,
　My Saviour and my Friend!

JESUS, MY LORD, MY GOD.

JESUS, my Lord, my God, my all,
　Hear me, blest Saviour, when I call;
Hear me, and from Thy dwelling-place
Pour down the riches of Thy grace.
　Jesus, my Lord, I Thee adore:
　Oh, make me love Thee more and more!

Jesus, alas! too coldly sought,
How can I love Thee as I ought?
And how extol Thy matchless fame,
The glorious beauty of Thy name?
　Jesus, my Lord, I Thee adore:
　Oh, make me love Thee more and more!

Jesus, what didst Thou find in me
That Thou hast dealt so lovingly?
How great the joy that Thou hast brought!
Oh, far exceeding hope or thought!
 Jesus, my Lord, I Thee adore:
 Oh, make me love Thee more and more!

Jesus, of Thee shall be my song,
To Thee my heart and soul belong;
All that I am or have is Thine;
And Thou, my Saviour, Thou art mine.
 Jesus, my Lord, I Thee adore;
 Oh, make me love Thee more and more!

AT EVEN.

"At even when the sun did set, they brought unto Him all that were diseased."—St. Mark i. 32.

AT even, ere the sun was set,
 The sick, O Lord, around Thee lay:
Oh, in what divers pains they met!
 Oh, with what joy they went away!
Once more 'tis eventide, and we
 Oppressed with various ills draw near:
What if Thy form we cannot see?
 We know and feel that Thou art here.

O Saviour Christ, our woes dispel :
   For some are sick, and some are sad,
And some have never loved Thee well,
   And some have lost the love they had ;
And some are pressed with worldly care ;
   And some are tried with sinful doubt ;
And some such grievous passions tear
   That only Thou canst cast them out ;

And some have found the world is vain,
   Yet from the world they break not free ;
And some have friends who give them pain,
   Yet have not sought a friend in Thee.
And none, O Lord, have perfect rest,
   For none are wholly free from sin ;
And they who fain would serve Thee best
   Are conscious most of wrong within.

O Saviour Christ, Thou too art Man ;
   Thou hast been troubled, tempted, tried,
Thy kind but searching glance can scan
   The very wounds that shame would hide ;
Thy touch has still its ancient power ;
   No word from Thee can fruitless fall ;
Hear, in this solemn evening hour,
   And in Thy mercy heal us all.

THE BLESSED SERVICE.

How blessèd, from the bonds of care
   And earthly fetters free,
In singleness of heart and aim
   Thy servants, Lord, to be!
The hardest toil to undertake
   With joy at Thy command,
The meanest office to receive
   With meekness at Thy hand:

With willing hearts and longing eyes
   To watch before Thy gate,
Ready to run the weary race,
   To bear the heavy weight:
No voice of thunder to expect,
   But follow calm and still,
For love can easily divine
   The One Belovèd's will.

Thus may we serve Thee, Gracious Lord!
   Thus ever Thine alone,
Our souls and bodies given to Thee,
   The purchase Thou hast won.
Through evil or through good report
   Still keeping by Thy side,
By life or death, in this poor flesh
   Let Christ be magnified!

How happily the working days
  In this dear service fly!
How rapidly the closing hour,
  The time of rest, draws nigh!
When all the faithful gather home,
  A joyful company!
And ever where the Master is,
  Shall His blest servants be!

WHEN THE DAY OF TOIL IS DONE.

WHEN the day of toil is done,
  When the race of life is run,
Father, grant Thy wearied one
    Rest for evermore!

When the strife of sin is stilled,
When the foe within is killed,
Be Thy gracious word fulfilled—
    Peace for evermore!

When the darkness melts away,
At the breaking of Thy Day,
Bid us hail the cheering ray;—
    Light for evermore!

When the heart by sorrow tried
Feels at length its throbs subside,

Bring us, where all tears are dried,
        Joy for evermore!

When for vanished days we yearn,
Days that never can return,
Teach us in Thy love to learn
        Love for evermore!

When the breath of life is flown,
When the grave must claim its own,
Lord of Life! be ours Thy crown—
        Life for evermore!

HELP THOU MY UNBELIEF.

MY sins have taken such an hold on me,
    I am not able to look up to Thee!
  Lord, I repent; accept my tears and grief:
But Thou hast taken all my sin away,
And I in Thee dare now look up and pray;
  Lord, I believe; help Thou mine unbelief.

Of nights unhallowed, and of sinful days,
Of careless thoughts, and words, and works,
    and ways,
  Lord, I repent; accept my tears and grief;
And in the Life which doth within me live,
And the forgiveness which can all forgive,
  Lord, I believe; help Thou mine unbelief.

Of selfishness which makes the soul unjust,
Envy and strife, and every sinful lust,
   Lord, I repent; accept my tears and grief;
And in the Blood, which doth my pardon plead
The Truth and Love, which for me intercede,
   Lord, I believe; help Thou mine unbelief.

Of sins that as a cloud have hid Thy face,
Of Thy care slighted, and Thy grievèd grace,
   Lord, I repent, accept my tears and grief;
In love which puts sin's envious veil aside,
Rending the veil of flesh which for me died,
   Lord, I believe; help Thou mine unbelief.

Sin is my sorrow, passion is my pain,
To Thee their vileness, and in me their stain;
   Lord, I repent; accept my tears and grief:
Christ is my joy; and out of all distress
He doth deliver with His righteousness;
   Lord, I believe; help Thou mine unbelief.

COME UNTO ME.

"COME unto Me, ye weary,
   And I will give you rest."
Oh, blessed voice of Jesus,
   Which comes to hearts opprest!
It tells of benediction,

Of pardon, grace, and peace,
Of joy that hath no ending,
　　Of love which cannot cease.

"Come unto Me, ye wanderers,
　　And I will give you light."
Oh, loving voice of Jesus,
　　Which comes to cheer the night!
Our hearts were filled with sadness,
　　And we had lost our way,
But morning brings us gladness,
　　And songs the break of day.

"Come unto Me, ye fainting,
　　And I will give you life."
Oh, cheering voice of Jesus,
　　Which comes to aid our strife!
The foe is stern and eager,
　　The fight is fierce and long;
But Thou hast made us mighty,
　　And stronger than the strong.

"And whosoever cometh,
　　I will not cast him out."
Oh, welcome voice of Jesus,
　　Which drives away our doubt!
Which calls us very sinners,
　　Unworthy though we be
Of love so free and boundless,
　　To come, dear Lord, to Thee!

A PRAYER.

So grant us, Lord, our race to run,
    That run we not in vain ;
And none Thy chastening rod refuse,
    And none His cross disdain.

Safe, keep us, gracious Lord, beneath
    The shadow of Thy wing ;
So shall we peaceful rest secure
    From every hurtful thing.

So grant us, Lord, our race to run,
    That run we not in vain ;
And all Thy glorious face behold,
    And all the crown obtain.

THE BEAUTIFUL GATE.

Lord, open the door, for I falter ;
    I faint in this stifled air,
In dust and straitness I lose my breath ;
This life of self is a living death :
    Let me into Thy pastures—broad and fair—
To the sun and the wind from Thy mountains free ;
Lord, open the door to me !

THE BEAUTIFUL GATE.

There is a holier life, and truer
    Than ever my heart has found;
There is a nobler work than is wrought within
These walls, so charred by the fires of sin,
    Where I toil like a captive blind and
        bound:—
An open door—to a freer task
In Thy nearer smile I ask.

    Yet the world is Thy field, Thy garden;
        On earth art Thou still at home;
When Thou bendest hither Thy hallowing eye,
My narrow work-room seems vast and high,
        Its dingy ceiling—a rainbow dome:
Stand ever thus by my narrow door,
And toil will be toil no more.

    Through the rosy portals of morning,
        Now the tides of sunshine flow
Over the earth and the glistening sea,
The praise Thou inspirest rolls back to Thee.
        Its tones through the infinite arches go;
Yet crippled and dumb, behold me wait,
Dear Lord, at the beautiful gate.

    I wait for Thy hand of healing—
        For vigor and hope in Thee:—
Open wide the door,—let me feel the sun,—
Let me touch Thy robe; I shall rise and run

Through Thy happy universe, safe and free,
Where in and out Thy beloved go,
Nor want nor wandering know.

Thyself art the door most holy!
By Thee let me enter in!
I press towards Thee with my failing strength:
Unfold Thy love in its breadth and length!
True light from Thine let my spirit win!
To the saints' fair city—the Father's throne—
Thou, Lord, art the way alone.

From the deeps of unseen glory
Now I feel the flooding light:
O rare, sweet winds from Thy hills that blow!
O river, so calm in its crystal flow!
O love unfathomed — the depth, the height!
What joy wilt Thou not unto me impart,
When Thou shalt enlarge my heart.

To be made with Thee one spirit,
Is the boon that I lingering ask,
To have no bar 'twixt my soul and Thine;
My thoughts to echo Thy will divine;
Myself, Thy servant for every task;
Life! Life! I may enter through Thee, the door—
Saved, sheltered for evermore.

"TO-DAY I MUST ABIDE AT THY HOUSE."

YEA, enter in, Thou gracious Guest,
    Lowly and poor my home;
Yet where Thy welcome footsteps rest,
    Riches and beauty come.
Fairer than sheen of palace walls,
The radiance of Thy presence falls.

For Thee my humble board I spread;
    Scanty and mean my fare;
But where Thy smiles of love are shed,
    Are viands rich and rare.
My bread becomes as manna fine,
And water turns to choicest wine.

No treasure rare and strange have I
    My peerless Guest to show;
Yet purest pearls around me lie,
    And priceless jewels glow:
Entranced, I view the wondrous store
That entered with Thee at my door.

I scarce may dare, with speech of mine
    Thy answering words to win,
But when my glance is raised to Thine,
    Thou readest all within;

And strains flow forth so pure and sweet,
I sit in rapture at Thy feet.

How can I hope to *please* my Guest?
　　To *serve* is all I try;
Yet when, to do some mild behest,
　　On eager wing I fly,
And haste again, to meet Thy smile,
How radiant has it grown the while!

Happy, indeed, the roof wherein
　　My Lord this day doth rest,
More happy, if it might but win
　　Him for a constant Guest.
Lord, in the heart I open wide,
Enter, and evermore abide.

𝕭𝖍𝖊 𝕻𝖎𝖑𝖌𝖗𝖎𝖒 𝖙𝖍𝖊𝖞 𝖑𝖆𝖎𝖉 𝖎𝖓 𝖆 𝖑𝖆𝖗𝖌𝖊 𝖚𝖕𝖕𝖊𝖗
　𝕮𝖍𝖆𝖒𝖇𝖊𝖗, 𝖋𝖆𝖈𝖎𝖓𝖌 𝖙𝖍𝖊 𝕾𝖚𝖓𝖗𝖎𝖘𝖎𝖓𝖌.
　　𝕿𝖍𝖊 𝖓𝖆𝖒𝖊 𝖔𝖋 𝖙𝖍𝖊
　　　𝕮𝖍𝖆𝖒𝖇𝖊𝖗 𝖜𝖆𝖘
　　　　𝕻𝕰𝕬𝕮𝕰.

INDEX TO SUBJECTS.

A Little While	244
A Little Way	20
Adoration	145
Alpha and Omega	250
An Evening Prayer	191
Anywhere	162
Art thou Weary, art thou Languid?	196
Aspiration	98
Aspirations	186
At Even	265
"Babes Always"	49
Beautiful Gate, The	272
Beleaguered Soul, The	254
Beyond	18
Best	65
Blessed Healed, The	220
Blessed Service, The	267
Border Land, The	198
"Bowing to God's Will"	158
By Thee, Jesus, will I Stay	221
Chamber of Peace, The	5
Chastisement	248
Closet Prayer	140
Cleansing Fires	184
Come unto Me	270
"Comfortable Words"	256
Coming, The	91

Communion Hymn	172
"Conformity to Christ"	246
Consolation in Christ	120
Cui Bono	133
Day	141
Difference, The	156
Dying, yet Behold! we Live	15
Endurance	147
Enticed	108
Every Day	180
Faith	176
Faith and Light in the Latter Days	151
Fainting Heart, The	195
"Far Away"	111
Fisher, The	227
"Follow Me"	77
For Saturday Night	103
Gathering Home, The	42
Gethsemane	117
"Give us this Day our Daily Bread"	238
God hath His Plan for Every Man	145
God Knoweth Best	114
Got not Far from Me	207
Going to Sleep	46
Good-Bye	60
Grow not Old	179
Hardest Time of All, The	75
Heart Ventures	177
Heavier the Cross	38
Heaven over All	133
Helpless	215
"He Leadeth Me"	121

INDEX TO SUBJECTS.

"He Careth for You"	225
"He Knoweth ye have Need"	165
He Knoweth All	33
Hereafter	72
Help Thou my Unbelief	269
Hope's Song	93
How Long	157
Hymn, A	81
Hymn of Faith	58
Hymn of Rest	56
I am His and He is Mine	61
I Thirst	101
I Stand and Knock	124
I and my Burden	132
I Gazed upon the Bitter Cross	175
I will Follow Thee	262
"I shall Die Alone"	51
If I should Die To-Night	99
"If God shall Bless me So"	57
In the Evening	11
"It is I; be not Afraid"	67
Jesus, my Lord, my God	264
Jesus Only	149
"Jesus, Help Conquer"	89
"Keep me from Falling"	234
Land Beyond the Sea, The	21
Last Hours, The	85
Lattice at Sunrise, The	59
Lay of Peace in Sickness, A	104
Lead Thou me On	231
Left All	142
"Let us Pass Over"	126
Looking Seaward	95

INDEX TO SUBJECTS.

Longing for Christ	54
Lord, Help Me	182
Loved and Lost, The	35
Lovest thou Me?	201
Mater Dolorosa	17
Mine Eyes shall See Thee	252
Mountain of Myrrh, The	154
My Cross	129
My Comforter	242
My Cross	138
Night and Day	14
Night-Watch, The	52
None or All	82
Not Now	218
Nothing	106
Oh, Weary in the Morning	205
Old Age	136
One Year More	101
One Step More	242
One of the Sweet Old Chapters	40
Other Shore, The	47
Our High Priest	153
Our Father Knoweth	262
Over my Dead	44
Peace	79
Peaceable Fruit	222
Penitential Hymn	167
Perfect Day, The	174
Pilgrim's Prayer, The	130
Prayer, A	272
Pray Without Ceasing	87
Praying in Spirit	127
Prayer for Rest in Sickness, A	213

Present Saviour, A	233
Preventing Mercies	168
Protest, A	245
"Purifieth Himself even as He is Pure"	113
Rest	122
"Remember not the Sins of my Youth"	148
Rest	171
Rest from the Burden	211
Rest in God	223
Rest	251
School Life	193
"Sealed"	128
Secret, The	24
Shadow of Death, The	159
Silent God, The	178
Sleep	40
Some Time	229
"So He Bringeth them unto their Desired Haven"	25
Song in the Night, A	97
Song of Abel in Heaven, A	235
Sorrow	12
Sparrow's Text, The	129
Strife and Victory	239
Straight Way, The	260
Sufferer's Couch, The	163
Sympathy of Jesus, The	204
Teach me to Live	216
Thorn and Cross, The	115
"Though I be Nothing"	54
"Thou art Near, O Lord"	259
Their Thoughts and Our Thoughts	118
Tired	9
Tired Mothers	63
'Tis all the Same to Me	29

INDEX TO SUBJECTS.

To-Day	105
"To-Day I must Abide at Thy House."	275
Transverse and Parallel	88
Trust	26
Twilight	185
'Twill Not be Long	70
Two Cities, The	30
WAITING for the King	164
Waiting for Jesus	189
Wandering	84
Watch	68
When the Day of Toil is Done	268
What Then?	34
When the King Comes In	236
Why Walk in Darkness	143
Will of God, The	28
Written on Recovery from Illness	73
"I shall Die Alone"	51
If I should Die To-Night	99
"If God shall Bless me So"	57
In the Evening	11
"It is I; be not Afraid"	67
JESUS, my Lord, my God	264
Jesus Only	149
"Jesus, Help Conquer"	89
"KEEP me from Falling"	234
LAND Beyond the Sea, The	21
Last Hours, The	85
Lattice at Sunrise, The	59
Lay of Peace in Sickness, A	104

INDEX TO FIRST LINES.

A sparrow lighted chirping on a spray	129
A little elbow leans upon your knee......MRS. ALBERT SMITH.	63
A little way—I know it is not far	20
A ship, full laden, left her native port	15
Across the discord of our lives comes lowly.ELLIE A. JEWETT.	165
After the burden and heat of the day	5
Ah, Lord! to be	186
All day the wind had howled along the leas	11
All goeth but God's will!......ALICE WILLIAMS.	28
Any little corner, Lord	162
Art thou worn and heavy-laden......L. D. M.	256
Art thou weary, art thou languid	196
As Mary knelt, and dropped her tears	167
As on my bed at dawn I mused and prayed..REV. C. TURNER.	59
At even, ere the sun was set	265
Because of little low-laid heads all covered...MARY K. FIELD.	17
Bend down from heaven, Almighty Love......V. A. R.	185
Beset with foes, like some beleaguered city......C. L. S.	254
Beyond life's toils and cares	18
Brother, called by Christ's name are we......G. Z. G.	236
By Thee, Jesus, will I stay......J. B. W.	221
Chafed and worn with worldly care	103
Come, all ye weary, worn, and sin-defiled	56
"Come unto Me, ye weary"	270
Could I recall the years that now are flown	148

(283)

INDEX TO FIRST LINES.

Dark is the sky that overhangs my soul	174
Do I not love Thee? Thou whose patient feet. ..... M. N. M.	201
Does the road wind uphill all the way?	9
Down through the hushed and thickening air..C. M. CADELL.	101
Faint not beneath thy burden, though it seem	147
Fling down the faded blossoms of the spring	136
Fold up thy hands, my weary soul............ROSE TERRY.	122
Go not far from me, O my strength ......MISS A. L. WARING.	207
God sends sometimes a stillness in our life...LUCY FLETCHER.	211
God's almighty arms are round me	104
Good-bye, good-bye, it is the sweetest blessing	60
He sees when their footsteps falter, when their hearts grow weak and faint	40
He took them from me, one by one ....F. H. MARR.	114
Heavier the cross, the nearer heaven	38
How blessed, from the bonds of care............C. J. FROST.	267
How many hours of patient toil...	133
I know not if the dark or bright	26
I cannot think but God must know..........."SAXE HOLM."	81
I have wandered to the mountain ....H. C. HOGDEN.	84
I gathered flowers the summer long	91
I hear it singing, singing sweetly	93
I stand and knock, at holy Advent time	124
I need not leave the jostling world...........HARRIET M'EWEN KIMBALL.	127
I am Thine own, O Christ.........................H. M. B.	128
I go on pilgrimage. The road in view	130
I and my burden, O Master	132
I love my God, but with no love of mine	145
I gazed upon the bitter Cross, and sought........ "ELPIS."	175
I thank Thee, Lord, that Thou hast kept ......ADELAIDE A. PROCTOR.	176
I sat in the school of sorrow	193

INDEX TO FIRST LINES.

I have been to a land, a Border Land	198
I have been dumb, and held my peace ......C. M. N.	248
I stood and watched my ships go out	177
If any consolation be ....H. L. HILDRETH.	120
If I could only surely know ....D.	225
If I were told that I must die to-morrow...SUSAN COOLIDGE.	85
If I should die to-night	99
In a valley centuries ago	93
In years long past, I said, "If God shall give"	57
In " pastures green?" Not always; sometimes He	121
In silence of the middle night......GEO. W. BETHUNE, D.D.	97
Is this the peace of God, this strange, sweet calm? FRANCES RIDLEY HAVERGAL.	79
It is not heavy, agonizing woe.	138
It is Thy will, my Lord, my God	73
"JESUS, I wait!" Last words breathed soft and low SARAH DOUDNEY.	189
Jesus, my Lord, my God, my all ......JOSEPH BARNEY.	264
Jesus, help conquer!	89
"KEEP me from falling!" ....F. A. L.	234
LET thy gold be cast in the furnace	184
"Let us pass over!" We were far astray	126
Like Him, whilst friends and lovers slept.................M. BERTHAM EDWARDS.	117
Long did I toil, and knew no earthly rest	61
Lord, I had planned to do Thee service true...... CAROLINE M. NOEL.	215
Lord, I have shut my door	140
Lord, I desire to live as one ....C. L. S.	246
"Lord, I will follow Thee," I said ....MARGARET J. PRESTON.	82
Lord, it is Thou! and I can walk......MISS. A. L. WARING.	67
Lord, a whole long day of pain	213
Lord, open the door, for I falter	272
MADE for Thyself, O God!	171

Master, unto Thy feet my gifts I bring.......................
                    MRS. MARGARET E. SANGSTER. 142
Men send their ships, the eager things 156
Mine eyes shall see Thee, O my Friend, my Sov'reign .C. L. S. 252
Mother, I see you with your nursery light...............H. H. 65
My Father, can I learn so hard a task?................E. J. A. 54
My Father! God of life and light....................M. L. B. 191
My God, it is not fretfulness................. 157
My sins have taken such an hold on me........................ 269
My spirit longs for Thee ....J. BYROM. 54
My silence and my solitude............. ....C. M. N. 244
My will, dear Lord, from Thine doth run...................... 88

NEVER, my heart, wilt thou grow old!..MRS. LOUISA J. HALL. 179
"Not clear, nor dark," not rain nor shine................... 141
Not *now*, my child,—a little more rough tossing..... ...C. P. 218
Not from the flowers of earth 72
Not worthy, Lord, to gather up the crumbs..................
                  REV. EDWARD H. BICKERSTETH. 172
Now while Thy hand is on me, O my God........:.......... 44

O HEART, that sad and weary 195
O Jesus, I have promised ....SAMUEL REAY. 262
O Jesus, Merciful! bend down..................... C. M. N. 251
O Lamb of God, I know that Thou art here ....A. S. 250
"O Lord, my God!" I oft have said........................ 129
O lead me on; the way is dark without Thee................
                    REV. H. B. WARDWELL. 231
O to be nothing—nothing!................ 106
O meditation sweet that makes...HARRIET M'EWEN KIMBALL. 52
O trifling task so often done ....ELIZABETH AKERS ALLEN. 180
O'er all the world the church spire rocks.REV. WM. M. BAKER. 178
Oh! come to the bedside in silence ......RACHAEL G. ALSOP. 46
Oh, linger sweet to-day!...... 105
Oh, weary in the morning.................................... 205
On the dusky shores of evening, stretched in shining peace it
   lies.. 30

INDEX TO FIRST LINES.

One of the sweet old chapters....	40
Only to-day! dark looms to-morrow....MRS. M. E. C. BATES.	238
PALE star, if star thou be, that art	133
"Pray without ceasing," says the zealous Paul............	87
SERENE I lie in Jesus' hands....................S. T. W.	242
Six years have faded since she went away............... REV. J. W. CHADWICK.	118
So grant us, Lord, our race to run...........................	272
"So!"—through storms and darkness.....JENNIE HARRISON.	25
Some time, when all life's lessons have been learned........	229
Sorrow, and strife, and pain .... SARAH DOUDNEY.	227
TAKE this maxim home to your heart	145
Take the praise we bring Thee, Lord	98
Teach me to live! 'Tis easier far to die.....	216
Ten thousand times ten thousand sung.......	235
The hawthorn hedge that keeps us from intruding........... HUGH MACMILLAN.	168
The vision fades away.. .... H. L. L.	149
The thorn is very sharp, O righteous Master................ SIMEON TUCKER CLARK.	115
The fretted waters of the bay................................	95
The Master's voice was sweet	77
"The loved and lost!" why do we call them lost............	35
The twilight falls, the night is near	33
The winds are raging o'er the upper ocean.................. HARRIET BEECHER STOWE.	24
The way seems dark about me; overhead..	182
The land beyond the sea!	21
The day is Thine...	14
There came an angel to me in disguise ...MARY E. ATKINSON.	239
There is a secret place of rest	204
There are days of deepest sorrow	75
Therefore, our Heavenly Father ....M. R. J.	262
They are gathering homeward from every land.............	42

INDEX TO FIRST LINES.

Thou sayest, "Take up thy cross"	FRANCIS T. PALGRAVE.	151
Thou in whose garden I have grown apace		101
Thy way, not mine, O Lord	HORATIUS BONAR, D.D.	260
'Tis all the same to me	PROF. THOS. C. UPHAM.	29
'Tis late—in my lone chamber	"MARION HARLAND."	49
To live and not to die		163
Touched with the feeling of our need!		153
Tossing at night upon a stormy sea		58
'Twill not be long—this weary commotion		70
UNDER the shadow of Thy wings, my Father	R. A. R.	223
Up to the fair myrrh mountain	HORATIUS BONAR, D.D.	154
Upon the shore		111
Upon my lips she laid her touch divine		12
"WATCH! for ye know not the hour"	SOPHIE E. C. DOWNING.	68
We sit alone in the stillness		164
We sometimes think that had our lot been cast		233
Weary, half weary of the work of life.	DINAH MULOCH CRAIK.	159
What though before me it is dark		242
What is it like—that other shore?	MARIANNE FARNINGHAM.	47
What then? Why then another pilgrim song		34
What shall Thine "afterward" be, O Lord	M. R. J.	222
Whate'er God wills, let that be done		158
When the world is brightest	R. R. CHOPE.	259
When across the heart deep waves of sorrow		220
When in deep silence my expectant heart	FRANCIS COLE.	113
When the rich gold and purple of Life's sunset		51
When the day of toil is done	C. C. SCHOLEFIELD.	268
Why press we so against the door that Fate.	CAROLINE NORTH.	245
Why walk in darkness? Has the clear light vanished	H. BONAR.	143
With what clear guile of gracious love enticed		108
YEA, enter in, Thou gracious Guest		275

www.ingramcontent.com/pod-product-compliance
Lightning Source LLC
Chambersburg PA
CBHW032101220426
43664CB00008B/1097